the TRUTH about relationships

Human & Rousseau

First published in 2016 by Human & Rousseau,
an imprint of NB Publishers, a division of Media24 Boeke (Pty) Ltd,
40 Heerengracht, Cape Town, 8001.

Copyright © published edition: Human & Rousseau (2016)
Copyright © text: Stefan Blom (2016)

No part of this book may be reproduced or transmitted in any form or by any electronic or mechanical means, including photocopying and recording, or by any other information storage or retrieval system, without written permission from the publisher.

Commissioning editor: Lindy Samery
Editor: Angela Voges
Proofreader: Tiara Walters
Design: Melanie Kriel
Cover and illustrations: Stefan Blom

Printed and bound through Creda Communications, Epping II, South Africa

ISBN: 978-0-7981-7207-3
EPUB: 978-0-7981-7208-0
MOBI: 978-0-7981-7209-7

the TRUTH about relationships

STEFAN BLOM

Human & Rousseau

To my parents,
for the gifts of awareness, creativity and truth.

contents

FOREWORD	12
INTRODUCTION	13
CHAPTER 1: Get ready to talk	17
THINK BEFORE YOU SPEAK	17
KNOW WHERE YOU ARE	17
THE SEVEN STEPS TO CONNECTION	19
Step 1: Stop the damage now	20
Step 2: Have some compassion	26
Step 3: Choose a time and place	27
Step 4: Protect your relationship	29
Step 5: Calm down	31
Step 6: Check your perceptions of each other	34
Step 7: Create a respectful space for talking	35
CHAPTER 2: Speak your truth (honesty and gently)	39
THE BENEFITS OF HONESTY IN RELATIONSHIPS	41
RELATIONSHIP SKILLS	43
Share your upsets	43
Decide what really matters	45
Introduce your need to speak	46
Take turns to speak	47
Show real interest	48
Speak only for yourself	49
Put the topic on the shelf	50
Stop trying to fix, and start trying to understand	51
Accept that you are different	52

CHAPTER 3: Know how to disagree	**57**
WHAT NOT TO DO	60
Don't fight to be right	60
Don't keep quiet	61
Stop making excuses	62
Don't fight about the facts	63
Stop reacting to each other	64
Don't lean on each other's fences	65
WHAT TO DO	65
Prioritise your relationship	65
Stop the escalation	67
Share your upsets responsibly	68
Speak only for yourself	69
Never compromise	70
EMERGENCY RELATIONSHIP TOOLS	72
Put the topic on the shelf	72
Talk about what you need	73
Extend an invitation to change	74
Speak to each other as if you are not alone	75
Find a good therapist	76
IN CLOSING	76
CHAPTER 4: A break in trust	**79**
THE MEANING OF TRUST	81
YOUR SACRED AGREEMENTS	81
WAYS TO BREAK TRUST	84
Our first wound	84
Our second break in trust	86
The obvious betrayal of trust: the affair	86
The every-day breaks in trust	89
Reactions to a break in trust	89
Why people break the agreements in their relationships	90
THE TRAGEDY AND THE IRONY	92
HOW TO RESTORE TRUST ON YOUR OWN	93
Adjust your expectations	93
Check your agreements	94

Set some boundaries	94
Put an end to the fantasy: speak the truth	94
Take a new position silently and strongly	95
HOW TO RESTORE TRUST WITH YOUR PARTNER	**96**
Have lots of honest conversations	96
Reach a clear, complete understanding of why it happened	96
Show willingness to be open about any aspect of the truth	97
Never call your partner overly sensitive or emotional	98
Sit with both parties' emotions in a calm and kind way	98
Offer constant affirmations and reassurances	98
Show affection	99
Have complete transparency about the tools used for the deceit	99
Show some appreciation	99
Relinquish control	100
THE TRUSTING RELATIONSHIP	**101**
Know where you stand with each other	101
Behave consistently over time	101
Stay committed to change	101
Focus on the place where words and actions meet	101
Treat each other with respect	102
IN CLOSING	**102**
A new relationship with new commitments	102
Take back your perceptions	103
Renew your vows	103
CHAPTER 5: Sex and intimacy	**105**
UNDERSTANDINGS OF SEX AND INTIMACY	**105**
Sex	106
Intimacy	108
The complex relationship between sex and intimacy	109
WHERE TO START	**110**
Change starts with a conversation	110
WHAT TO DO	**117**
Stop making excuses	117
Stop being sexually lazy	118
Change your physical space	119

Make sex and intimacy your priority	120
Share your fantasies	120
Change your sexual focus	121
Kiss, kiss, kiss	122
Get naked	122
Stroke and caress each other	123
Connect your mind and body	123
Make yourself more attractive	124
Know your erogenous zones	126
Increase your intimacy	126
Go on regular dates	128
Increase your romance	128
Work around the not-so-sexy roles	129
IN CLOSING	131
CHAPTER 6: Dating (and meeting new people)	**133**
THE FIRST ROUND	133
AWARENESS IS YOUR PROTECTION	134
For starters, use that checklist	134
Understand the layers of attraction	135
At the heart of your future	136
PREPARING YOURSELF FOR DATING	138
What is dating really about for you?	138
Dating as social research	138
Are you ready for dating?	139
Do you like yourself enough to be liked and loved?	140
Are your boundaries strong enough?	140
Are you ready to step outside your comfort zone?	141
Can you spend time on your own?	141
Which dating method do you prefer?	142
How would you like to present yourself?	144
LESSONS LEARNT	145
A 'maybe' is a 'no'	145
Age is relevant	146
Distance as a deal-breaker	146
Substances create false connections, sometimes	146

Income is relevant	147
You need, or are, what you are attracted to	147
Your generosity is never a problem	147
Your emotions never lie	148
Charm is a skill	149
Potential is not reality	151
Moving too fast causes accidents	152
Children as a deal-breaker	152
Real interest needs no questions	153
Inconsistency means constant upsets	153
Bullies, princesses and narcissists are real	154
Words and actions should always be consistent	154
Emotional shallowness exists	155
Takers are not givers	155
Emotional unavailability: don't go there	155
IN CLOSING	156

CHAPTER 7: Loving yourself	**159**
CHANGE THE WAY YOU SPEAK	160
Question your ideas about yourself	161
Define yourself with awareness and truth	162
Speak the truth about who you really are	164
Start developing a new inner voice that is kind and gentle	166
CHANGE WHAT IS AROUND YOU	169
LEARN TO COMFORT YOURSELF	172
CHANGE WHAT YOU DO	173
Stop worrying about what people think of you	173
Switch off the television	174
Get to know your area	175
Be grateful for what you have	175
Make some good memories	175
Change your physical space	176
Learn to deal with your moods and temper	176
Take charge of your depression or anxiety	177
Look at your hormone levels and thyroid function	177
Laugh a little, or a lot	178

Spend time in nature	178
Keep a journal	178
Breathe, sweat and move	179
Eat good food	179
Walk	179
Drop a bad habit	180
Step outside the patterns of your every-day life	180
Get some sleep	180
Spend time in or near water	181
Invite people into your life	181
Climb a mountain	181
Step outside of time	182
Listen to music	182
Garden	182
Cook	183
Read a good book	183
Surround yourself with creativity	183
Slow down	184
Be here, now	184
DO WHAT YOU SAY	185
IN CLOSING	187
CHAPTER 8: Ending a relationship	**191**
BEFORE YOU END YOUR RELATIONSHIP	191
A real change	192
WHY RELATIONSHIPS END	194
How you speak to and treat each other	195
Constant fighting and disagreement	195
A lack of emotional connection and understanding	196
A loss of trust	196
Failure to prioritise your relationship	197
A loss of attraction	197
Too many outside influences	198
Addictions	198
Different sexual preference or orientations	198
ONE LAST CHANCE	199

THE END OF A RELATIONSHIP	199
Why do we keep going back?	199
THE END IS THE END	202
End all contact	202
Stop avoiding your emotions	203
Stop the blame	203
Comfort yourself	204
Remember what is true about you	204
Seek the company of friends and family	204
Try to make sense of what has happened	204
Take your pain to nature	205
Get out	205
Seek some help	205
IN CLOSING	205
EPILOGUE	**208**
CHAPTER 9: Questions and answers	**211**
TRUST	211
SEX AND INTIMACY	213
DISAGREEMENT	214
DATING	215
CONDITIONS	218
CHANGE AND GROWTH	219
FINANCES	222
THE LIFE OF A RELATIONSHIP	223
LOVE	232
GRATITUDE	**233**
ABOUT THE AUTHOR	**234**

foreword

*I am in love and I am lost
But I'd rather be
Broken than empty
Oh, I'd rather be
Shattered than hollow
Oh, I'd rather be
By your side*

First Aid Kit, 'Shattered and Hollow'

My words feel like a gift that needs to be given. They are the words I have spoken for many years to couples and individuals in therapy, and the words I have learnt from many people struggling to make sense of their relationships. They are also what I have learnt from being in relationships myself. For many years, I have written them in notebooks, on my laptop and phone, and on little scraps of paper. Often, before I fall asleep at night, or when I am with couples in therapy, jogging, with my family, or walking on the beach, the truth about relationships comes to me like a light in the dark. As I have written and spoken these words over the years, I have seen how they have moved people and changed their lives.

I hope my words will give you direction, ideas and – above all – relief.

introduction

The experience of your relationships determines the experience of your life. This is a simple truth. If you feel close and connected to the people around you, life feels good.

Connection is the highway to happiness.

A life without real relationships is not a good life. The truth is that real relationships are honest and connected relationships – there is no other way to be in relationships. A life with close and connected relationships is always a more meaningful and significant life.

In our core, we are made for real connections. Our basic human nature is designed for togetherness, closeness and connection.

Animals and humans crave feeling connected to one another, because we feel incomplete without closeness and connection. When you don't feel close to your daughter or son, or when you feel distant from your partner, it makes you unhappy. If you connect only with things and places, you don't feel complete. To be truly happy, we need real, connected relationships.

To connect and stay connected is to love.

Because we are designed for real connection, there is no other way but to live an honest and connected life. A real relationship is an honest relationship. The closer you are to the people and animals around you, the happier you will feel. Being connected is happiness in action.

The only life worth living is a life of honest, close connections.

We remember and cherish our moments of true connection. When we speak about the times when we were truly happy, we speak about the moments when we felt more connected to ourselves and the people around us. These are the best times of our lives, for the simple reason that the more connected we feel to ourselves and the people closest to us, the happier our lives feel. When you look at an artwork, your pet, your partner, your garden, or your parents, and you truly connect with them, you love them. In these moments of true love, you will move and be moved, and life will bring you real joy.

Real, connected relationships hold the power of happiness. Maybe relationships are all that matter. Maybe relationships are all we really have to give us joy.

How often you are honest and connected to yourself and the people around you will determine the experience of your life. Think about it.

Our connections to places, things, people and animals need to be honest and real. We all know that connections to things and places are not as powerful as connections to humans and animals. The ironic truth is that the more things you have, and the more beautiful the place you are in, the more your need for real connections will surface. When we are in beautiful places, we miss our real connections. Therefore, we find true happiness in our relationships with the people and animals we connect with and love.

In the next nine chapters, you will find ways to move from disconnection to connection in any of your relationships. These include:
- Steps you can take to prepare yourself and create a context for having honest conversations;
- A selection of basic relationship skills that you can use for speaking honestly and openly;
- A selection of advanced relationships skills that you can use during your most difficult conversations, especially when you disagree;
- Practical steps to restore a sense of trust in any of your relationships, if trust has been broken;
- Exercises and topics for discussion that could assist you to reconnect sexually and intimately;
- A collection of questions in preparation for dating, and lessons for dating and meeting new people;
- An understanding of what you can do, practically, if your relationship feels like it is ending or when your heart is broken because your relationship has reached its end; and …

- An honest and practical guide to how to love yourself;
- Some frequently asked questions, with answers.

This book is written in such a way that you can read any topic of interest to you. At the same time, you may learn something about yourself even when you read a chapter that does not seem to apply to you.

Chapter 1
get **ready** to **talk**

You may think you need to express every upset you feel, but being upset does not mean that you have to start speaking. If you are upset, you should rather start thinking. We can benefit greatly from thinking before we speak – reflecting before we react.

THINK BEFORE YOU SPEAK

What are you thinking about? Think about what you see in yourself and in your relationship. Focus on observing yourself and your relationship, instead of always looking at your partner. Before you start speaking and reacting, first think about what is really going on inside you and in your relationship.

You cannot change something you do not see.

If you don't know where you and your partner are in life, you will be disconnected from yourself and the person closest to you. Not knowing where you are in yourself and your relationship holds risks for you and your relationship.

KNOW WHERE YOU ARE

Staying connected to yourself and your relationship means knowing where you and your partner are emotionally, intellectually, spiritually, financially and sexually most of the time. If you lead a busy life, it is, of course, not always possible to know this exactly. Couples and individuals who do not check in with themselves on a regular basis will find themselves disconnected and in trouble over time.

Knowing where you are with each other means staying connected.

At times of disconnection, it seems more important to know where you are than to know who you are. In a way, we know who we are, but we don't seem to know where we are in our lives.

Do you know what you are thinking and feeling at this point in your life? Do you know what you need for yourself and your relationships? Do you know what matters to you … what is really important to you in life?

Do you know where you partner is nowadays? Do you know what is on your partner's mind and in his or her heart? Do you know how he or she is really doing, and what he or she needs?

If you don't know, you might be in trouble.

It is good to know where we are in life. When you can see where you are, and where you partner is, you feel seen and acknowledged. And being seen feels like love. You are connected to yourself and your relationship when you can truly see where you are, or where your partner is. When we feel seen, we feel loved.

To see and be seen is to love and be loved.

To see more of yourself, your relationship and each other, work through some of the following questions to get a sense of where you are.

Questions to ask yourself

The following questions might guide you in thinking about yourself:
- What do I need in life?
- Where am I emotionally, physically, financially, sexually or spiritually?
- Which part do I play in the 'upsets' in my relationship? How do I think I have contributed to the upsets in my relationship?
- What do I think I could have done differently that could have helped and improved my relationship?
- What are some of my best contributions and what am I proud of when it comes to my relationship/s?
- What am I trying to do to contribute to the well-being of my relationship?
- Why do I think I behave in my relationship as I do?
- What are my true intentions when it comes to my relationship?
- What am I hearing and what am I struggling to understand?
- What am I trying to say?

Questions to ask about your relationship
The following questions might guide you in thinking about your relationship:
- What is it like to be in our relationship nowadays?
- Which experiences of our relationship do I/we dislike?
- Which experiences of our relationship do I prefer? How would I/we like our relationship to be?
- What am I/are we contributing to the life of our relationship?
- How can I/we improve the experience of being in our relationship?

Questions to ask about your partner
The following questions might guide you in thinking about your partner:
- What do I see when I look at my partner's behaviour?
- What is my partner really feeling and thinking?
- What is my partner really trying to say to me?
- Why is he or she thinking and feeling like this?

When you reflect on your life, it is good to make mental or physical notes. While you have thoughts about yourself and your relationship, consider writing them down on your phone or laptop, or in a journal. Making notes of thoughts and feelings is, for most people, a good tool for observing their lives. In this way you don't have to hold your thoughts in your memory, and will have clear ideas of where you are.

THE SEVEN STEPS TO CONNECTION

After some thinking, it is time for some doing. Real change does not happen through thought alone – it happens through thought and action. If you want to change the experience of your relationship, take action now, before you destroy your love for each other.

If you are feeling unhappy in your relationship and disconnected from yourself and the people you love, and you are stuck in a damaging pattern of fighting, take any of the following seven steps to start reconnecting:

Step 1: Stop the damage now

We have all been there.

You pick up a topic, and try your best to share what you think and feel about it. Soon, you are screaming and shouting, or walking away. You feel even more hurt and upset in that moment; neither of you really feels understood. You feel disconnected, unloved, distant and stuck. You don't feel safe enough to be honest with each other. The atmosphere is tense, sometimes for days – until you have the courage to try again, only to find the same pattern repeating itself. You learn to keep quiet and live separate lives. You start sharing your inner thoughts and feelings with friends or family members; the distance grows until you feel like strangers living together or co-parenting.

In times of disconnection, we seek comfort. We create a false sense of love and intimacy by creating comfort zones. You spend more time at work, or with friends and family. You spend your evenings in front of your laptop or the television. You learn to live in the same space, but avoid any real sharing. This is what it means to put your relationship at risk.

Most couples ask me how to break this pattern. They feel stuck, lost; they do not know how to become unstuck. How is it possible to be upset and speak your mind, but still feel close? How can we break this horrible cycle of fighting and silence?

In case you don't know how to have a conversation without damaging each other, this is not the way to talk to anyone, ever. Whether you are in an intimate relationship or not, speaking to anyone like this is not good for you or your relationships.

If you damage your relationships, you damage yourself.

Before you start talking, remove all the ways of speaking that damage you and your relationship. Just as you would clean a wound before you put a plaster on it, you need to cleanse your relationship of your damaging ways before it can heal.

If the way in which you speak or behave is doing damage, rather do or say nothing and learn, first, how to treat each other with respect. If you cannot speak with gentle respect, do not speak at all until you are ready.

The best conversation you can have is a conversation that causes as little damage as possible.

Most couples fight more about how they speak to each other than about what they say to each other. What they say is often less damaging than how they say it. The way in which you speak your mind will determine the outcome of your conversations. The sooner you stop your damaging ways, the better for your relationship.

A damaging conversation is one in which you:
- scream or shout at each other;
- use sharp or sarcastic tones;
- call each other names or use labels ('you are stupid/ridiculous/ oversensitive/crazy');
- shove, scratch, or hit each other, or push or pull each other around;
- slam doors and cupboards, or break things;
- use silent treatment and refuse to speak as a form of punishment (passive-aggressive behaviour);
- withhold your love and your thoughts, refusing to participate or show interest;
- swear;
- interrupt each other;
- threaten your relationship or say things you don't mean ('I am not doing this any more!', 'You will regret this one day!'); or
- make general, sweeping statements you don't really mean ('You always do this!', 'You never do anything!').

Despite the fact that we all know we are not allowed to speak to or treat each other in these ways, most couples struggle to keep it gentle, calm and respectful.

Why do we raise our voices and scream at each other when all we want is to be heard? Why do we keep fighting when we know it doesn't work? Often, I find that the more misunderstood you feel, the more you raise your voice. We shout to be heard. We fight to be seen and to be understood, because we believe that if we truly love and respect each other, our partners will understand and show interest in our thoughts and feelings.

This ugly, destructive fighting makes me wonder: are you not interested in what you partner really thinks and feels? Is it so important for you to be right that you cannot hear your partner? Why do we continue to treat each other in such a damaging way if we know it never works?

We fight for our right to be heard and seen.
We should never fight to be right.

We know how to fight, how to hurt each other and damage our relationships. I don't know about you, but no one has ever spoken to me about how to talk, how not to talk, and how to disagree with love. All we do is try, desperately, to be understood and seen. When you partner really gets what you are saying – when you feel seen – you feel loved and respected. In that moment, you feel calm again.

The three biggest mistakes couples make when they disagree are:

Interrupting. Most couples feel that they will forget their thoughts if they don't articulate them the moment they have them. Of course, interrupting each other damages your relationship even more. The obvious solution to interruption is simply to take turns, and to make notes if you are worried that you won't remember what you wanted to say when it is your turn to talk.

Screaming and shouting. In the classic screaming match, one partner says, 'Stop screaming at me!' and the other, 'I am not screaming at you … I'm talking loudly.' In a funny kind of way, we have all been there – arguing about arguing. When couples ask me, 'Do you think I am screaming?' the answer is simple: 'If your partner thinks you are screaming, to him or her you are screaming.' You need to honour your partner's experience. You don't have to agree, and you don't have to like it, but you do have to accept that it is too much for you partner. If you respect his or her experience, you will tone it down.

On a scale of one to 10, one person's volume tolerance may be three, and another's eight – maybe because this person is Italian! Whichever way, your tolerance or sensitivity to volume is determined by how much sleep you have had, your hormones, what you had for breakfast, how your parents used to argue – and many other factors. It is a simple truth that when your partner says your voice is too loud, it is too loud for him or her. You need to respect this and tone it down.

Your sensitivity or tolerance to volume or tone should never be debated, simply respected.

Avoidance or walking away (the silent treatment). This is the other side of the screaming-and-shouting coin. It can be as damaging as screaming and shouting, and is its silent form. After an upset or a disagreement, you simply refuse to participate. You sulk and throw silent tantrums like a child, avoiding an adult-to-adult conversation. It can be very painful to feel that you are in trouble without knowing why. Nobody likes to live in silence and tension that lasts for days. The obvious solution is to say what you want to say as soon as possible, and not to act it out. When you are upset, you should speak your mind.

In relationships, there is a point of no return – a point at which your damaging ways start to destroy the core experience of your relationship. Your fights can destroy your love and respect for each other. So, get to know your pattern of destruction as soon as possible and promise each other to try your best never to speak to each other like that again. Only you can end it and then find a new way of speaking that celebrates your love.

Ending the damage that destroys your connection is one of the most important steps in any relationship. You need to come to a new agreement about your relationship that commits you to refrain from speaking to each other in ways that do not honour your love. Committing to this sacred agreement restores respect and trust in your relationship. Your intention is always to speak with love and respect. Do not argue about this agreement – rather accept your preferences without judgment or argument and always regard the agreement as important and relevant. Simply make a list of all the unacceptable behaviours in your conversations and agree that you will try your best to no longer behave in these damaging ways. Your promises form a new, sacred agreement, and your relationship will not survive if you do not honour it.

It is because we are imperfect human beings that we have imperfect conversations. Your intention is never to be perfect, but rather to try your best to have the best conversation you can have. To have conversations that bring you closer to each other, you need to be honest, calm and open to hearing and understanding each other.

Your intention is to stop hurting each other and start hearing each other.

If your imperfect human ways are damaging each other, you need to try harder. Take as many turns as you need to speak to each other with love and respect. You don't have to be good at making conversation – you just need to be honest and non-damaging to the best of your ability.

If you make a mistake, such as screaming and shouting, claim your part in the damage. Apologise for your destructive contribution and try harder next time.

The intention is not to have a positive conversation, but a real and honest one. It is not about positive speaking, but honest, gentle speaking. It's about talking, not screaming.

The way in which you engage with each other is at the heart of the experience of respect and commitment in your relationship. Your commitment to each other comes from the way in which you speak to each other. How you speak to each other will determine whether your love, which is built on respect and commitment, will grow or fade away. For this reason, you have to take it very seriously and watch how you speak. Always.

Questions to ask yourself
- How does the way I talk and behave in my relationship cause damage?
- Where do I need to work on myself to be less damaging in our conversations?
- In which ways do I behave that I am not proud of in my relationship?
- How would I like to behave instead?

EXERCISES FOR YOUR RELATIONSHIP

Exercise 1: Make a list of damaging behaviour
Without blame or finger-pointing, make one list of all the damaging behaviours in your relationship (past and present) that you no longer want. This is not your chance to start a fight. Start by speaking for yourself first. You both get a turn to add one behaviour at a time that you would like to remove from your relationship, to create a list of damaging behaviours that you are both responsible for preventing in the future.

Exercise 2: Define how you would like to speak to and treat each other instead
Now, speak about how you would like to speak to and treat each other. Define a new way of speaking, disagreeing and being that would be good for your relationship. Here are some questions to guide you:
- How would we like to speak to and treat each other instead, from this day forward, which would demonstrate love and respect for each other?
- Which ways of talking and behaving do we prefer?

Exercise 3: Make a commitment to a new way of speaking
Make a promise (written or verbal) to each other that you will try your best to keep your damaging ways out of your relationship. Show your commitment to a new way of speaking and being in the future by writing it down. Speak about what you will do if you break a promise. If you speak to each other in damaging ways again, you need to apologise and talk about it. Questions to guide you include:
- What are the terms of our new commitment to each other regarding speaking and behaving?
- What do I promise to you and our relationship?
- What will we do if we break our promises to each other?

Step 2: Have some compassion

Look beyond the person who is upsetting and hurting you and ask yourself:
- Why is this person treating me like this?
- How is this person really feeling?

The person who is speaking to you in damaging ways is most likely in pain. There is no need to damage other people, so the person who is doing so is neither okay nor happy. This person may believe that he or she has the right to speak to people in such a damaging way. Whatever he or she is thinking or feeling, the truth is that people do not like themselves when they speak to each other in damaging ways. In simple terms, doing so does not make anyone feel good.

The truth is that if you damage others, you also damage yourself. What you do to others, you always also do to yourself. What you are getting is a smaller share of what this person is giving to himself or herself. People who judge or criticise you are often so much more critical of themselves. The person who neglects you is also neglecting himself or herself.

Having compassion for the person who is treating you in damaging ways means that you have to look beyond your own experience and have a deeper understanding of why that person behaves in this way. Look beyond your own distress and think, with kindness, about what this person might be going through. This does not mean accepting each other's damaging ways – compassion simply allows you not to take all the damage that comes your way so personally, but rather to see it as the responsibility of another. A person who speaks to you in a damaging way is not your responsibility.

The truth is that no matter how you have behaved, others do not have the right to treat you badly. You do not have the licence to hurt or damage others just because you are in a bad mood, upset or unhappy. If you do damage to others, you need to take a closer look at yourself and ask yourself why you treat others in ways that also damage you. Nobody can do your work for you.

Being on the receiving end of another person's damaging ways with some compassion may help you to see a difficult interaction in a new way. It may shift your internal focus away from, 'What am I doing wrong?' to, 'Is this person okay? I wonder how he or she is really doing ...'

Here are some questions that could deepen your compassion for another person.

Questions to ask yourself
- Why is this person speaking to or treating me in this way (especially if I did nothing to provoke it)?
- What is this person really going through that makes him or her treat or speak to me like this?
- What is my responsibility (if any) in this damaging interaction, and what is not?

Step 3: Choose your time and place

Being upset and having something to say doesn't mean that now is the right time or place to say it. Feeling like talking doesn't mean that the conversation should take place at that moment, because 50 percent of the success of your conversation is in choosing the best time and place for talking.

It is never a good time to have a conversation if you are:
- intoxicated (after two or more drinks, or if you have taken drugs);
- exhausted;
- time pressured or in a hurry;
- hungry;
- hormonal;
- too upset or angry to keep your emotions contained;
- stressed;
- distracted; or ...
- simply not in the mood.

The worst places to have a conversation are:
- in your car (you don't have the option of leaving the conversation);
- in front of your children;
- in front of friends or family;

- in public;
- in bed or in your bedroom;
- when the television is on; or …
- when you are busy on your phone, laptop or tablet.

At times like these, you should learn to calm down, gather your thoughts and decide when you both think might be a good time to talk. In fact, when you are simply not in the mood for talking, you should not talk.

So, you might be wondering: when *is* a good time to speak? Most couples I meet live very busy, full and stressful lives. The secret is to book a time in your busy schedules for talking and create a safe space for doing so. In this way, you honour your love and respect your relationship by giving it the time and importance it deserves. This is what it means to prioritise your relationship: to give your relationship a moment in time, a moment in your busy lives, in which it gets your respectful attention above all else in your life.

Choose the time and place carefully, as these can make or break the conversation. This skill of choosing a time and place for talking can spare your relationship many unpleasant and damaging conversations.

Questions to ask about your relationship
- What is the worst time for you to have a conversation, and why?
- What is the worst place for you to have a conversation, and why?
- When would the best time be for you to have a conversation?
- What is your favourite place for talking?

AN EXERCISE FOR YOUR RELATIONSHIP

If you are always busy, tired and time pressured, and feel that you never have time for your relationship, you will need to book times for important conversations in advance. Ask:
- When can we make time to talk about things in our relationship?
- When will the best time be for us to talk?
- Then, make a date.

Step 4: Protect your relationship

It is important to look closely at what has affected you and your relationships over time. You may think there is something wrong with your relationship when, in fact, you are simply experiencing very stressful circumstances. Sometimes, life gives you something you didn't choose. This is simply life happening to you. And if you have control over what happens to you and your relationship, you should carefully consider what you allow into your life.

Exposing your relationship to too many outside influences can destroy your relationship from the inside.

Not everything that happens to you and your relationship is always under your control. You have control over your reactions, of course, but sometimes is it obvious that you didn't invite or choose a certain experience.

Outside influences that you do not choose include:
- any act of random violence or abuse (being attacked, abused or raped);
- the death of a family member or friend;
- illness or any medical emergency;
- accidents of any kind;
- uninvited interference from family and friends;
- professional demands that you cannot control; and ...
- losing your job (for reasons other than your own actions).

It is important to be honest about the effect of these uninvited influences on your life. There is no point in being hard on, and critical of, yourself if you didn't invite the influence into your life. At times like these, you should be kind and gentle to yourself and your relationship. It seems nonsensical to fight about an influence you didn't choose; life is stressful enough. This is the time to take better care of yourself and your relationship.

On the other hand, many outside influences *are* under your control.

Outside influences over which you have control include:
- your consumption of alcohol and drugs;
- financial stress or mismanagement;
- working long hours and burn-out;
- an affair;
- travel;
- opening your relationship to allow others into your intimate space;
- your relationship with family members and friends;
- living for others or worrying what they think about you;
- renovations or moving house;
- fame or public scrutiny; and …
- the space in which you live.

If you would like to feel more connected to yourself and your relationship, consider every influence on your relationship seriously. For example, not drinking for an extended period or taking a break from destructive people can be a good start.

The experiences with which you surround yourself become part of you.

When you feel stressed by what is around your relationship and not in your relationship, it is time to clean out and protect your relationship. Often, I am reminded that couples or individuals under tremendous stress would experience their lives very differently if they were not under so much stress. Feeling constantly overwhelmed, exhausted and stressed is your cue that you need a change, that it is time to take better care of and protect your relationship. One of the best steps you can take to protect your relationship is to close it, for as long as is needed, to negative outside influences. Slow down, create some private spaces and spend more time with yourself, your family and your partner.

Questions to ask about your relationship

Deepen your understanding of and compassion for each other and your relationship by looking closely at what really affects your relationship.
- What have been some of the biggest influences on our relationship?
- How have these influences affected our relationship and us?

- How can we support each other during this time?
- What can we do to change things?
- How can we protect our relationship from damaging external influences?

Step 5: Calm down

Being told to calm down when you are upset is, for most people, like a red rag to a bull. You may not like being told to calm down when you are upset, but the reality is that you need to be calm when you speak about your upsets.

Try to calm down before you speak

The couples I have seen over the years are usually very upset, hurt or angry when they walk into my rooms. But the truth is that you have to calm down before you speak, because the upset partner and the calm partner are often two different people!

Your goal is to have a conversation, not a fight

In order to speak your minds and not shout your minds, you need to calm down first. It is not anyone's responsibility to calm you down or tell you to calm down – you are always responsible for calming yourself down. If you don't like to be told to calm down, you should look at your own responsibility here. The reality is that no matter what is upsetting you, you are always responsible for keeping your side clean by staying calm.

How calm you both are when you start speaking determines the success of your conversations. Being upset is your cue that you need to have a conversation, and being upset does not mean that you have to fight. The question is: can you share, and not shout, your upset?

Every upset is an invitation to talk

Being upset is your relationship speaking and directing you. It highlights the need for a conversation. Every upset not shared is a missed opportunity for connection. Being upset is simply saying to you that you need to prepare your mind for a conversation.

The best conversations start in a calm, relaxed place. The simple truth is that if you are not feeling calm, you shouldn't speak. Calming down means observing yourself and your reactions and to stop being reactive. It is about learning to observe yourself and your relationship, gathering your thoughts and feelings, and not simply reacting to everything that comes your way.

Thinking about your relationship, instead of reacting to it, can create an instant sense of calm

The reality is that we have our best conversations about 'upsets' when we are ready and relaxed, which is why lots of couples pick up a topic for conversation when they are on holiday. As soon as we start to feel relaxed and feel that we have the energy and strength for a conversation, we try to speak to each other.

But life is not a holiday! We never have enough time, and always feel stressed and exhausted. From this place, we try to speak our minds ... share our inner thoughts and feelings. It's not surprising that most conversations turn into screaming matches.

So, what seems true is that feeling upset does not mean it is a good time to speak. Rather, it is a good time to try to gather your thoughts. The best conversations start from a place of calm and a time and place that are well considered. These two considerations will determine the life of your conversation.

If one of you is not calm, wait for both partners to calm down before you speak. Being calm does not mean that you are not upset. You are most likely not calm – you are most likely hurt and upset, and you have the right to be upset. But being upset does not give you the right to speak with disrespect.

Being hurt or upset doesn't give you the license to speak in a damaging way.

Calming down is easier said than done. At times like these, it is often a good idea to do more and speak less – to make conversation less important, and relaxation and enjoyment of your time together the real focus. When you find yourself enjoying your time together, you create an inviting context for speaking. Your chances of having a constructive conversation are much greater when the conversation starts from a good, calm place.

A good conversation requires energy and calm

The secret is to calm down first and recharge your energy level. Make sure that you have the energy for this conversation and that you are calm enough to express your inner thoughts and feelings. This is a time for reflection, not reaction. This seems to be a difficult skill for most couples, but it is one of the most important skills that anyone in a relationship can learn.

You often only gain real perspective when you step away and relax, and then look at your relationship

I often wonder, in therapy, why it is so difficult for couples to wait to have a conversation. Why is it so difficult to calm down first and then choose a good time to speak? One of the reasons is that couples have a history of trying to speak to each other, having things quickly turn into an ugly fight, and then giving up on the topic because they feel they are getting nowhere and are exhausted from trying. The promise to speak about it later is never kept. Neither of you trusts the words, 'Let's talk about it later,' because it never happens. The moment you have something to say feels like your one and only chance – one that you will fight to hold on to. So, for most couples, their partners saying, 'Not now, I'm tired' or, 'Can we speak about this later?' is infuriating. Most of the time, it is the end of the conversation and can often, therefore, feel like abandonment and rejection, even if it is not.

Questions to ask yourself
- How do I calm myself down when I am upset?
- How can I avoid causing more upset in my relationship when I am really upset?
- In a moment of real upset or anger, what can I do to calm myself down?
- How do I relax my mind when I am upset?

Step 6: Check your perceptions of each other

Often, what stands in the way of your ability to have a calm, non-reactive conversation is your perception of each other. It seems to be human nature to generalise about one bad experience and speak about it as if the person involved is always like this. If you lied, once, in one area of your life, you become a liar and cannot be trusted at all. If you spoke, once, in a damaging way, you become a bully or an abuser. Often, speaking to friends and family about our hurtful relationship experiences feeds and validates our generally negative perceptions of our partners. Like you, your friends validate your generally negative beliefs about your partner and feed your own general perceptions.

But, as humans, we are not general – we are specific. We are kind and, sometimes, not so kind. Be careful not to take one or two experiences in a specific area and generalise them. Trust is never broken in totality – it is broken only in a specific area. For example, I might not trust you with money, but I trust you with our children. Be specific about the behaviours you do not want and would like to change.

In an argument or conversation, your general perceptions of each other may stand in the way of hearing each other and having a calm and understanding conversation. Statements like, 'You always do this …' and, 'You never do that …' are signs that you are seeing your partner in general terms. Even if there is some truth to your perception, see if there is another side to your partner by checking your general perceptions.

Questions to ask yourself
- Which general beliefs do I have about my partner?
- Which of my beliefs about my partner are standing in the way of really seeing him or her?
- What is the truth about who he or she really is?
- What are my beliefs doing to our interactions?
- How can I correct my perceptions and avoid speaking in general terms?

Step 7: Create a respectful space for talking

Just as a bird builds a nest to hold a delicate egg, it is a good idea to build a nest for conversation into which you can put your sensitive topics. To build a nest is to create a context for speaking, a beautiful space that invites you to have a good conversation.

For starters, it is never a good idea to have a conversation while standing. Standing and talking does not show serious intent. Rather, it shows that you are on your way somewhere. To give your conversation the respect it deserves, it is best to sit down when you have it.

A couch or a table is a good place to start a conversation.

Sit on your couch or at your table, and start speaking. As simple as it might sound, it is not easy – we often feel upset or hurt in that moment. Remember that every time you are upset or hurt, or you disagree, it is an invitation to talk. By asking your partner to sit with you and talk, you indicate the seriousness and respect you intend to give your relationship.

Respect each other and your relationship by switching off or removing all electronic devices. No couple has ever managed to speak successfully in front of a television or computer screen.

Often, when you switch on an electronic device, you switch off your relationship. The intention is to switch on to each other and your relationship. It's also not good for your relationship to bring electronic devices such as televisions, phones and tablets into your bedroom. Intimacy and screens don't live well in the same space; screens should be banned from your bedroom.

> **AN EXERCISE FOR YOUR RELATIONSHIP**
> - Name the place where you would like to have a conversation with each other.
> - Tell each other why you prefer to have your conversation in this place. And promise your partner to invite them into this space when you have indicated that you would like to speak.

Once you have indicated that you want to speak, and have created a safe and comfortable place to do so, start talking. You are now ready to speak your minds.

Chapter 2
speak your truth
(honestly and gently)

Speaking your truths – that is, sharing your thoughts and feelings – is one of the best gifts that you can give your relationship.

A real conversation is a process in which two people share their thoughts and feelings honestly and gently and start feeling closer to each other. The best conversation you can have will move you from disconnection to connection, from tension to closeness.

One of the best ways of feeling a warm closeness is to speak from your mind and from your heart. That feeling of distance and disconnection is about all the things you do not say and this causes the tension in your relationship. Disconnection caused by not sharing honestly feels like tension in any relationship. The tension caused by disconnection is life's constant reminder to become honest. The quickest way to relieve yourselves of this unpleasant tension and distance is to share your truths. That feeling of disconnection is your invitation to share what is on your mind.

What you do not say to yourself and the people around you causes the distance and disconnection you feel.

All your thoughts and feelings that matter to you and that you are not expressing cause the tension and distance you feel in your relationship. Your unspoken words sit between the two of you like a rock on a narrow road. You cannot see each other, because there is so much in the way. When you start speaking about that rock, you start clearing your path to connection and closeness.

When you speak your truth, you free yourself of that heavy burden of having kept your emotions and thoughts to yourself for so long. It changes the experience of your relationship. As we are made for honest connection, we have an obligation to share what is on our minds and in our hearts. Even if hearing the truth is painful, at times, honesty has a powerful liberating effect. With the pain or hurt of truth comes relief, and movement towards a stronger connection. Real relationships are always honest relationships.

One of the main aims of any relationship is to speak your mind – to share your truths gently. Happy couples share their minds and hearts gently and honestly, and very regularly.

The best way to speak your mind is with honesty, kindness and gentleness.

Speaking the truth about yourself, your relationships and your life is not easy, yet we have no choice but to share our minds and hearts. The moment you have the courage to speak from your heart, you start moving from disconnection to connection.

It is not supposed to be easy: it is supposed to be honest.

You do not have to like what you hear. The conversation just needs to be honest, patient and very real. It is not easy to hear that you have upset or hurt or angered or disappointed your partner. Who likes to hear that? Honesty can bring you closer, but can also upset your relationship. But the upset that comes with honesty is never a problem, as it is part of the process of getting closer to each other. You need to expect, and learn to deal with, the upsets that come with honesty. This is one of the most important skills in any relationship: being honest, and dealing with the consequences of being honest.

THE BENEFITS OF HONESTY IN RELATIONSHIPS

Connection and closeness are two of the many benefits of sharing your truths.

When you feel distant or disconnected in your relationship, it often means that you are not getting what you need and are keeping quiet about it. If you speak you mind, you might get what you need and expect. If you don't say it, you don't get it, and you may remain full of unmet expectations. It is not your partner who is hurting or upsetting you – it is your own unexpressed expectations. Expectations are unexpressed, silent needs. When you talk honestly about what you expect, your expectations become needs. From that moment of truth – when you become truly honest about what you need – you will start feeling better, as you give each other a chance to participate in meeting each other's needs. A need that is not shared openly is a missed opportunity for happiness and connection.

When you share honestly, you move your relationship from a space of guessing to one of knowing. The things we think but do not share always leave us guessing, wondering, questioning and, sometimes, obsessing. When we don't know what is going on in a relationship, we tend to fill the spaces with doubts, assumptions and questions. Often you start with questioning your relationship and, in time, you start doubting yourself. Not knowing what is going on is damaging. So, you should be grateful when you partner tells you what he or she is really thinking or feeling, even if it upsets you, because then you know exactly where you stand. Clear, honest positions are always better for you than guessing what is going on.

It is more important to know than not to know.

Another benefit of honesty is growth and movement. Relationships can only survive and grow with honesty. How often you share your mind and heart honestly determines the life of your relationship.

If you don't speak the truth in your relationships, you will never get anywhere. You will always stay stuck in the same place.

If you are not interested in movement and growth, you are not interested in the future of your relationships. We all know that as you move through life, you change – that growth is inevitable. That your relationship will change as your life does is a fact of life.

Movement is love.

If you take the time to share your innermost thoughts with someone you love or want to love, and that person does not want to hear them, then he or she is not really interested in you. You need to ask yourself why. If happy relationships are all about sharing our minds and hearts, and if the person with who you are sharing is unable or unwilling to hear you, you need to ask, 'Why would a person who loves me or shows interest in me not be willing to listen to my mind and heart? Are we not in the kind of relationship in which honest sharing is allowed?'

The truth about relationships is that if you love each other, you will grow with each other through sharing. A relationship that does not move over time will not survive.

You have the right to share. You have the right to your feelings and thoughts.

If you are in a real relationship, you have the right to share what you think and feel. And if you want to be in a happy, honest relationship, you need to be willing to listen to what is being shared. If you are not interested in this process of sharing, you are neither interested in nor ready for a real relationship. What is the point of having a relationship that does not welcome sharing?

Your inner thoughts and feelings are always relevant to your relationships as they are a part of you – part of your identity. Therefore, they need not only to be heard, but embraced. It is a privilege to share the most private thoughts of the people around you; you need to show your respect in exactly the same way, as you would expect it to be shown in return.

When couples share their inner thoughts and feelings in therapy and one partner constantly interrupts the other or starts fighting, I ask:

- Are you not interested in your partner's thoughts and feelings?
- Is it not okay for you to listen to what you partner has to say?
- Do you not want to hear what you partner is really thinking and feeling?
- Would you not also like to be heard and understood?

In relationships, we feel and experience life in different ways. This is at the core of any relationship. We all carry different truths. Your main focus is to honour, embrace and see each other's different experiences. When you do, you truly see each other for who you are.

Relationships that do not consider what you think and feel – in which your experience is not important, and in which you don't try to 'see' each other – will make you unhappy. The reason is simple.

It is hurtful not to be seen.

So, when you share your thoughts and feelings, remind yourself that your main focus is to see and be seen. This is an experience of true love.

When we feel seen, we feel loved.

If you know what upsets you and what you need from your relationship, but have difficulty expressing it in a way that makes you feel understood and seen, you need to learn some relationship skills. These skills are important in all relationships, and anyone can learn them.

RELATIONSHIP SKILLS

If you struggle to share honestly and gently, the following relationship skills may guide you during your most honest and difficult conversations:

Relationship skill

Share your upsets

When we don't feel seen and acknowledged by the people we love, we get upset or feel hurt. Being upset and, at times, hurting each other is part of being in a relationship. Having good intentions, and loving and caring for each other deeply, do not mean that you will never hurt each other. Being upset is an important – and inevitable – part of being in a relationship.

Being upset means life is giving you direction.

When times are difficult and upsetting, I find that life is guiding you and your relationship. Your relationship is speaking to you if you are upset or hurt. It is telling you that you have to make time to share your inner thoughts and feelings. Being upset is your invitation to share your moment of truth. Every upset that you sweep under the carpet and ignore is a missed opportunity for connection.

The golden rule is that if you have a thought or feeling that bothers or upsets you, and you sleep on it and wake up the next day still feeling the same, it is relevant to your relationship. You need to discuss it. Every upset not discussed is a missed opportunity for connection. Be honest about what you think and feel, and share it gently.

The sooner you share your upsets, the better for your relationship.

The moment you feel upset, you need to remind yourself that a conversation might follow. The longer you keep your upsets to yourself, the more damaging it is for your relationship. This is called your 'turnaround time', and it is a skill. The time between feeling upset and sharing your upset will determine the experience of your relationship. Most couples I meet stay upset for days, months and even years. But the truth is that every day spent with upsetting thoughts and feelings is a wasted one.

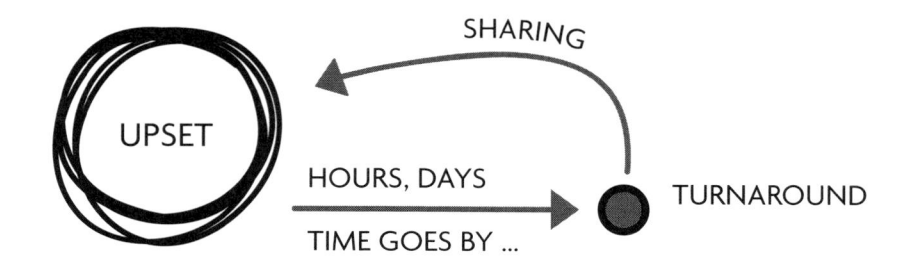

Even if your partner caused you to be upset, you are responsible for sharing your feelings with him or her. Your upsets are always your responsibility. You have a responsibility to the life of your relationship by sharing your upsets. Not speaking your truth inevitably creates a crisis, which will force its way to the surface like a ball that pops back up when you push it under the water. So, the next time you are upset, remind yourself to share it honestly and gently – as soon as possible.

Questions to ask yourself
The following questions might guide you in the process of sharing your upsets:
- What really upsets me in my relationship?
- What is important to me in my relationship at this point in my life?
- What needs to be shared or spoken about that I am keeping to myself? What is really going on inside me that I am not saying?
- What do I need or expect from my partner that I am not sharing?
- When I feel upset, how, when and where can I share my thoughts and feelings?

If you struggle to answer these questions, no longer know what is true for you, or feel so lost that you no longer have a sense of who you are, you should start the process of checking in with yourself. Looking closely at yourself is about seeing yourself and your relationship. When you are lost, it is good to write down your inner thoughts and feelings – writing is a good way of seeing. In time, you will experience what is really on your mind. Once you connect with what is true for you, you will never forget it. Once you have seen yourself and your relationship, you cannot pretend that you haven't. You cannot change what you cannot see. So, knowing yourself and your relationship is essential for changing your relationship.

Relationship skill

Decide what really matters
If you think it and feel it, it is your right and responsibility to share it. This doesn't mean that every thought or emotion is relevant and important. Sharing every thought and feeling would be an exhausting mistake. Instead, filter through your thoughts and share the ones that really matter to you and the life of your relationship. A simple rule

here is the sleep test. If you take a thought or feeling to bed and it holds the same intensity when you wake up the next day, it is asking to be shared. If keeping a thought or emotion to yourself will prevent growth in your relationship or cause tension, it needs to be shared.

If a conversation topic is important to you but not to your partner, it is relevant and important to your relationship. What matters to one of you may not matter to the other, but if you are in a relationship in which both of your experiences matter, you need to embrace them. Never fight about whether a topic is 'big' or 'small' – what is small for you may be big for your partner and, consequently, deserving of attention.

What matters to one partner should always matter to the relationship.

If you are scared to speak your mind because you expect a fight or an argument to result, or if you don't feel safe enough to do so, you need to start with the next skill: the skill of coming to an agreement about how, when and where to speak, or not speaking until you are ready.

Questions to ask yourself
- What is on my mind that is really important to my relationship and to me?
- Which point or issue needs more understanding in our relationship?
- Where do I feel really misunderstood or not seen in my relationship?
- Which point or issue would I like my partner to understand better?

Relationship skill

Introduce your need to speak
Sensitive topics need a well-chosen time and place for discussion and, often, a sensitive introduction. If you know that what you are going to say may upset your partner, no matter how gently you say it, introduce the conversation before you bring the topic up. When you introduce your need to speak about a sensitive topic, you prepare your relationship for a sensitive and possibly difficult conversation. Doing so gives everyone some time to prepare and connect with the seriousness of what might come. Your short introduction could sound like this:

'I would like to speak to you about … [name your topic]. I know this is difficult for you, but I think it's important that we speak about it.' You could also prepare for the conversation by sharing your intentions or why you would like to share this sensitive point. Although you cannot control the outcome of the conversation, you can speak about how you would like the conversation to go.

Questions to ask yourself
Asking yourself the following questions could help you during this process:
- Which topics are sensitive in my relationship?
- Why are they sensitive topics?
- How can I be more considerate about how I speak about my relationship's most sensitive topics?
- How can I introduce a topic that is sensitive to my relationship?

Relationship skill

Take turns to speak
When you share your upsets, you have to accept that you will need to take turns to speak about what is really in your hearts and on your minds, without interrupting each other or fighting. This is not an invitation to fight – it is an invitation to speak, to exchange your inner dialogues.

The best thing you can do for your relationship is to try, always, to have the best conversation you can have.

This conversation may not be a perfect conversation. Conversations are not meant to be perfect – they are meant to show interest in, and understanding of, each other's real thoughts and feelings. One of the best ways to have them is to give each other a turn to speak, respectfully.

A good conversation is not always a dialogue. A monologue – a conversation in which one person does most of the talking and the other listens and acknowledges – can be a very powerful process. If you struggle to listen without interrupting and fighting, try to take turns to do most of the talking. Try your best to listen and understand when it is not your turn to talk.

Questions to ask about your relationship
- Who wants to take the first turn to speak?
- How can we decide whose turn it is to speak?
- What can we do if we feel we might lose track of our thoughts while the other person is speaking?
- What can we do when we keep interrupting each other?

Relationship skill

Show real interest

Your focus in a conversation is, firstly, to show interest in your partner's real experience and, secondly, to understand what he or she is saying to you. Your focus should never be on being right or on fixing things or finding solutions, because real interest and understanding *are* the solutions.

The experience of a solution comes when you both feel seen, acknowledged and understood. That moment is a relief for most – the moment in which you see that your partner is really trying to understand you and is showing a real interest in what you are saying. Being seen is beautiful and it makes us feel deeply loved.

A willingness to try to understand each other's experiences of life is an act of love.

You show your interest in understanding, and your willingness to understand, by switching off your television or phone, giving your relationship your undivided attention and looking each other in the eye when you speak. Trying your best to show real interest and understanding in what is being shared is the best conversation you can have. Doing so will bring you closer and make you feel more connected to each other.

Questions to ask about your relationship
- Which of our behaviours during a conversation make us feel unacknowledged and unheard?
- Which of our behaviours during a conversation speak of real interest?
- Which promise can we make to our relationship in terms of how we will show real interest in the future?

Relationship skill

Speak only for yourself

Speaking your mind means sharing *your* ideas, thoughts and feelings, not your partner's. Be careful of telling your partner what he or she is feeling or thinking, as you are not the carrier of his or her heart or mind.

The best way to try, always, to speak for yourself is to start your sentences with 'I' instead of 'you'. So, instead of saying, 'You don't know what you are doing … you always say this to me,' consider speaking for yourself by saying, 'I need you to look at how you speak to me. I would really love it if you … ' When you speak for yourself, you stay in your lane.

Being spoken for is, for most people, deeply upsetting and often the start of a fight that goes nowhere. When you speak for another person, you could be assuming that you know best, or that you are always right. Of course, you are never right for both of you – you are only right for yourself, as your partner is only right for himself or herself. So, to put it simply, **you are both always right.**

Whereas you have the right to your own observations about each other and your relationship, it is irresponsible and disrespectful to speak for another. Claim what is yours and speak for yourself – you know yourself best. I am often reminded that you, having lived with your body, mind and soul for all the years of your life, have spent more time with this person called 'you' than anyone else. You certainly have more of an idea about who you are and what you like and dislike than anybody else in the world.

Nobody should speak for another person without his or her permission. If you want to comment on your partner's thoughts and feelings, it is good manners to ask their permission before you do so. Since you do not live in his or her body or mind, you simply cannot know what the person next to you is thinking or feeling.

Questions to ask about your relationship
- How can we remind each other to stay in our own lanes and speak only for ourselves?

▸ When we start speaking for each other, how can we get ourselves back to speaking only for ourselves?

Relationship skill

Put the topic on the shelf
This skill of not speaking when you feel or think something, but rather when you are ready, is called putting a conversation on the shelf or having a timeout. It involves putting the conversation to one side and picking it up later when you both feel prepared and calm enough to speak about it respectfully.

When you put a topic on the shelf because you are too upset, it is best to not leave it there for more than 24 to 48 hours. Often, it becomes too painful to wait any longer to speak, which becomes disrespectful to each other and your relationship. Your promise to each other is that you will pick up the conversation within the next day or two. The sooner you are ready to talk, the better.

Two practical skills really help couples to put a topic on the shelf. The first is putting a glass jar somewhere visible in your home, and dropping topics for conversation into it as they come up. In this way, you can see when a topic has come up for discussion, which you will need to speak about within the next day or two. Anything from household issues to deeper emotional points can be stored in the jar for picking up later.

The second is stating when you need to put a topic on the shelf or use a timeout – specifying, in that moment of upset, when would be good to talk. You could say, for example, 'I don't feel like talking now, but can we speak tomorrow morning at breakfast?' or 'I would love to hear what you have to say, but not now. Can we speak about it tonight?' Each couple must find their own way of doing this. The skill of putting a conversation on the shelf can save your relationship a great deal of exhausting and damaging talking.

If you don't like the idea of a jar for topics, you can simply indicate your need for talking by asking, 'When can we talk?' or, 'I need to speak to you' or, 'When would be a good time for us to sit down and talk?' Finding the courage to indicate that you need to talk needs to be respected and honoured with the best, most honest conversation you can have.

This is not a skill that you use to avoid conversations. It is a tool for protecting your relationship. It is an essential skill for stopping the damage in a moment of upset and a tool you use for taking better care of your relationship and each other.

The person who calls for a timeout is trying to protect your relationship, because – for whatever reason – the way in which you are speaking is too damaging or upsetting for him or her. You have the right to protect you relationship. The golden rule of the timeout is that the person who puts the conversation on the shelf is responsible for picking it up again within the next day or two.

If your partner indicated the need to talk and you called for a timeout, it is your responsibility to pay attention to the topic and give it the time it deserves. It is disrespectful to ignore what matters to your loved ones; doing so can even be seen as a lack of commitment, respect and love.

Questions to ask about your relationship
- What would be the best way, in our relationship, to put a topic on the shelf?
- What would we prefer to say to each other when we want to put a conversation on the shelf?
- Which ways of putting a conversation on the shelf would not work for our relationship? Why?

Relationship skill

Stop trying to fix, and start trying to understand
Intimate relationships, involving emotions, are different from business and all other relationships. In work relationships, there might be right and wrong problems that have obvious solutions. But you cannot treat your intimate relationships like work relationships, as your intimate emotions and thoughts are deeply personal and influence the way you perceive and feel things.

How you perceive the world reflects your identity – your personality. Work is often about goals, outcomes, productivity, results, competition, money and performance; relationships are about intimacy, connection, sharing, honesty, respect, understanding, individuality and togetherness. Your intimate relationship lives in a very different world from your business relationships, and has different rules of engagement. You cannot treat your intimate relationships like you treat your business relationships.

Personal and intimate relationships are never about fixing things and finding solutions. For most couples, this is difficult to understand. They see a problem in their relationship and want to find a solution to it, to fix what is wrong. The 'fixing' of your relationship lies in seeing and understanding each other's most private experiences. Trying to fix each other and your relationship, rather than trying to see and understand each other's experience of life, can often feel disrespectful.

Fixing your relationship involves truly showing interest in and an understanding of each other's experiences of life.

To be seen and feel love, we need to accept each other's very different experiences as true. What is true for me – my experience – does not have to be true for you. You have the right to your own, and often very different, experience of the same events.

Questions to ask about your relationship
- What is my intention for fixing and finding solutions for each other?
- If one or both of us slip into the old habit of trying to fix or find solutions for each other, how can we support each other in not doing so?
- What does it mean to try to understand each other, as opposed to fixing or finding solutions for our relationship?
- How can we support each other in our attempts to understand each other?

Relationship skill

Accept that you are different

We need to accept that no two people will see the same thing in the same way. We should allow each other our different experiences, and be really interested in how we experience the world differently. In a way, we should seek to disagree. Disagreement means that two or more people have taken the time and courage to share their most important thoughts and feelings, and feel so strongly about them that they refuse to agree. Couples who never disagree may be keeping quiet about what they really think. Sweeping your real thoughts and feelings under the carpet has never proven to be good for any relationship.

If you see the world differently to your partner, and feel strongly about how you see it, no amount of dialogue will make you see the world in the same way as your partner.

So, the secret is to move away from fighting to be right and to accept that you are right for only you. What is right for you may not be right for your partner. It simply cannot be true in a relationship between two people that your experience is the only experience and, therefore, the right one. The reason is logical: you are two people viewing the world, not one. Rather focus on accepting that **you are both always right**, because your experience is your experience and your partner's experience is his or her experience. No amount of dialogue or debate is going to change that.

Remember that people have different views and equal rights to express them. If you don't believe that you and your partner have equal rights to express yourselves or have your own opinions, you will never be truly happy. A relationship in which you cannot honestly speak your mind will never be a happy one. The truth is that if you don't want to hear your partner's position, you don't want a real relationship.

Be mindful of the following:
- People usually have different perspectives or opinions of the same event.
- You have the right to your opinions and experiences of life. And, of course, you have the right to share your views and speak your mind.
- Nobody's experience of life is the only right experience, ever. You are both always right, because you both experience life in a way that is right for you.
- If you fight to be right, you will both always be wrong, and 'lose'.
- You need to respect each other's different views. You don't have to agree or like what you hear, but you have to try your best to show interest in and understand each other's views.
- If you are not interested in seeing and understanding your partner's views, you do not respect him or her, because how you see and experience life is a reflection of your identity.
- Your past relationships, you parents' relationship, how much you slept last night and what you had for breakfast can determine how you view an event. Why can you not simply accept that you have different views about life and that you do not always need to be right?
- You are not a reaction to your partner's reactions. His or her damaging behaviour doesn't give you the right to do damage as well. You are responsible for your own reactions, not your partner's.
- No matter how your partner behaves, you always have a responsibility to keep it calm, gentle and respectful.
- Speak for yourself. Avoid using sentences that start with 'you'; rather speak for yourself with 'I' statements.
- Most couples fight about how they speak to each other, forgetting about what they started fighting about. The way in which you speak your mind often overshadows what you are speaking about.
- The aim of an adult-to-adult conversation is to show interest in and understanding of each other's experiences of life. Interest is your first step; real understanding comes with practice.

Questions to ask about your relationship
- How can we remind each other that we are both always right?
- How can we support each other to hear our different views?
- What can we do to support each other when we start fighting because we think we are right?

It is because we are so beautifully different that we have to learn one of life's most important skills: how to disagree.

Chapter 3
know **how** to **disagree**

The way in which you disagree affects your commitment and attraction to each other – it also ultimately affects how much you respect each other. It is no wonder that learning how to disagree is one of the most important skills for any relationship.

I'm right.   No, I'm right.

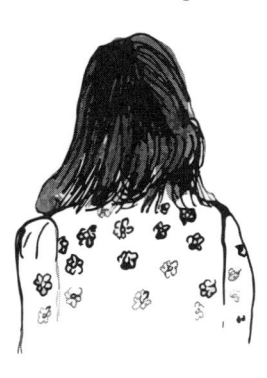

When you share your truths and encounter a difference in opinion or perception, you disagree. Disagreeing is good for your relationship as it is the first step on the path to feeling connected. Speaking your truths, even if you disagree about them, could move you towards the closeness that brings happiness to your relationship. It is a simple truth: you cannot be happy if you do not share what is on your mind and in your heart, and if you do not know how to disagree.

Disagreement is the essential skill of a real relationship.

Many couples ask me how to disagree, because how they are doing it at home is not working. They are stuck in a pattern of picking up the same topic over and over again, only to drop it in the exhaustion and frustration of fighting. They want to know how to break this pattern and become 'unstuck'. How do you disagree and get to a place where you both feel truly understood? How do you disagree and still feel your love?

Disagreeing and still feeling loved and connected is a skill that anyone can learn. When I sit with couples in therapy, it is clear to me when they can see each other and when they cannot. I witness how couples struggle to accept that they are different, and that they view life differently. But, isn't it okay for us all to have different views? Why do we all need to see and feel things in exactly the same way all the time?

A disagreement is an opportunity to get to know each other.

When you disagree, be grateful that your partner has had the courage to speak his or her mind, despite the risk of conflict. One person has had the courage to speak up and share some inner thoughts and feelings. This should be embraced and respected.

To maintain a level of respect during a disagreement, be mindful that you both have the right to your own needs, preferences, ideas, thoughts, feelings and experiences, and that it is your basic human right to share your experiences in your relationship and in the world. One of the main aims of a disagreement is to understand that both of your perspectives are equally important. You tell me what you think and feel, and I tell you what I think and feel. We take turns; we create a beautiful, safe, honest space for speaking and sharing, which is what it means to respect each other and your relationship.

You should never aim to agree; rather aim to be honest.

When you are honest, you don't have to like what you hear. A disagreement is an invitation for a beautiful, honest conversation. It is an invitation to share your minds. It is a moment of truth where both your opinions are of equal importance. Why should we not want to share our most important thoughts and feelings with the person we consider most important?

Learning to disagree is about learning how to accept two opinions in the same space. For every two people speaking their minds in a disagreement, there are two truths. The main aim of a disagreement is to create a safe space where both your truths can live comfortably. Instead of aiming to agree, spend your energy on understanding each other's very different truths.

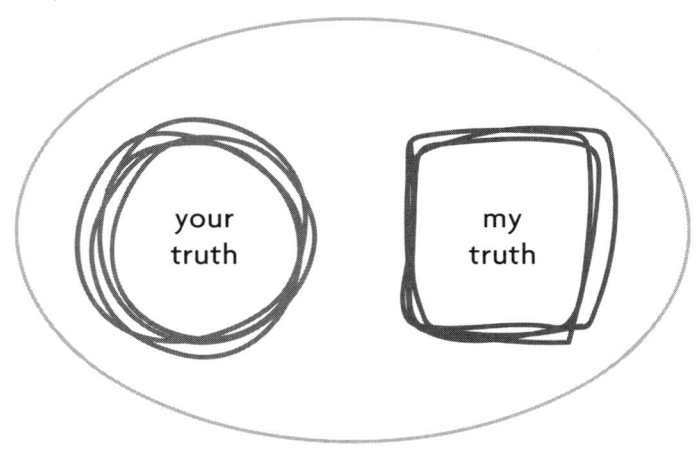

your truth

my truth

When I hear two people describing their opinions and feelings about the same event or topic, it often sounds like I am listening to two completely different stories about the same event. It brings to mind the image of two people standing near a large sculpture or painting and talking about how they experience it, with one looking at it from one perspective and the other from another perspective. Both will tell you what they see and how it makes them feel.

If they both believe they are right about how they see the work of art, and the other person is wrong, they are going down the wrong path. If they give each other the space to speak about what they see and feel, they both win. This is how we are supposed to disagree: sitting together and looking at the same thing, from different perspectives, and giving each other the space to have, and share, our own experiences.

Your truth is not the only truth.

Yet we struggle to be comfortable with a difference in opinion. Why do we struggle to allow each other to be different? Why can't we have different opinions? We have to be 'more right'. I am right, and you are wrong, and if I shout what I think loudly enough, you will hear me. And so, a disagreement quickly turns into a fight. In our pursuit of being right and winning the fight, we show our ugly, imperfect sides, using raised voices, sharp tones, or silence to win over our partner. Even if the fight ends with our partner agreeing with our point of view, the victory feels hollow. Why?

We don't want to be wrong. A disagreement should never be a competition, but a chance to be seen. Fighting dirty to get your point across leaves no one feeling like a winner. And if you both fight to win, you both lose. Always.

WHAT NOT TO DO

During a disagreement, adhering to the following don'ts works for most couples.

Don't fight to be right

How often you can speak your minds honestly and how comfortably you can accept your differences determine the experience of being in your relationship. If you don't know how to disagree, your relationship might feel like a series of screaming matches and fights.

A disagreement is never a fight.

Every disagreement that turns into a fight slowly destroys the core of your relationship. But sharing your truth gently, even if it is difficult for your partner to hear, is a step in the direction towards connection. A relationship with more healthy disagreement and fewer fights is a happy relationship. The truth is that life is too short not to speak your mind in your most important relationships.

Unfortunately, the way in which we disagree creates more problems and causes damage and distance. We have all been there: picking up an issue and trying to hear and understand each other, but starting to fight, or giving up ... feeling even more confused and misunderstood. As easy as we all think it is, it seems most of us do not know how to disagree.

The aim of a real conversation is not to win or to be right. This is the biggest mistake that couples make. You try to convince your partner and argue your point to be right. And this way always makes both parties feel even more misunderstood. It is at times like these when couples start screaming to be heard. The more you scream and shout, the less it means that you are listening.

If you start to fight because you disagree, you miss an opportunity for honest conversation, one of the most powerful pathways to connection.

I wonder, sometimes, what we are fighting about, what we are fighting for, and what it would take for us to allow our partners to have their own views and for us to be okay with it. In a world of multiple perspectives, of interesting, diverse ideas and thoughts, there is always more than one truth.

Questions to ask about your relationship
- When we start fighting, what are we trying to achieve?
- What are we fighting for?
- When our talking turns into fighting, how can we stop?
- When one of us believes we are right and the other is wrong, how can we remind each other that we both have the right to our perspectives?

Don't keep quiet

A disagreement is an invitation to understand each other – to get to know each other. But, even though we know this, we fear the consequences of speaking our minds. Because most disagreements lead to conflict, uncomfortable silences and exhausting fights, we don't speak our minds.

You might think that keeping quiet is better than fighting dirty. But keeping quiet is the other side of the fighting coin, and is just as damaging. It is the silent version of screaming your thoughts and feelings. Keeping quiet about what you really think, or walking on eggshells, is not good for your relationship. It often means that you don't feel safe enough to share your thoughts and feelings.

Questions to ask yourself
▸ How can I remind myself not to keep quiet, and to speak about what I really think and feel?

Questions to ask about your relationship
▸ What can we do to make our relationship a safe place, so that we can feel comfortable with sharing our minds?
▸ How can we support and encourage each other not to keep quiet, but to share more in our relationship?

Stop making excuses

Often, we avoid the real issues by making excuses. The three most common excuses couples use are:

'We don't have time'
Using the excuse of a lack of time, or of being too busy, most likely *does* mean that your life is too full and busy. But continuing to say this to each other without changing anything will get your relationship into trouble. Relationships do not wait for you. You are the driver and creator of the experiences of your own relationship and time does not fall from the sky. The truth is that nobody will give you the time you need. You need to make the time and the best way to do so is to book time in advance in your busy schedules for your relationship. When you give your relationship time, you prioritise your relationship over all other activities in your life. Giving your relationship time and space is essential for the survival of any relationship.

'I am Mediterranean, Latin-American, Italian, emotional or passionate'

The fire in your veins does not give you permission to behave in damaging ways. You cannot use your passionate or emotional nature as an excuse for disrespecting others. If you know you are passionate or emotional, or that you have a short fuse, you need to be even more mindful about how you speak. Using your origins and nature as an excuse speaks of not taking responsibility.

A temper that is constantly out of control is often about deep-seated insecurity masked by a big ego. Your reactions to your insecurities manifest in your disrespect for others, but are ultimately about your disrespecting yourself.

'We are too stressed'

Stress is one of intimacy and connection's biggest enemies. You have a responsibility to protect your relationship from stress. Hiding behind the excuse of stress means that you are not taking care of yourself or your relationship. Too much stress for too long can extinguish the flame of your relationship. Therefore it is important to make time, consciously, for relaxation and enjoyment.

Questions to ask about your relationship
- What are the most common excuses we make in our relationship?
- What are our excuses doing to our relationship?
- What do we allow into our relationship when we make excuses?
- How can we stop making excuses and take better care of our relationship?

Don't fight about the facts

When you disagree, you have different thoughts and feelings about a topic. You are not on the same page, can be full of strong emotions, and want to be heard and understood.

When you see things differently, you feel them differently too. And because when we disagree there is such a mixed bag of strong opinions and emotions, it can seem impossible to distinguish between fact and emotion.

Perceiving things with strong emotions often changes the facts about them.

You will seldom view what happened exactly in the same way as your partner. So, fighting about the facts, or how we feel about things that have happened, is a waste of time.

Fighting about your perception of how things happened will only make things worse. Use your energy, rather, to accept that you disagree and aim to understand each other's very different views.

Questions to ask about your relationship
- When we start disagreeing about the facts, how can we change direction and accommodate both of our perspectives?
- How can we remind each other that both of our versions are always right for us?
- How can we become comfortable with disagreeing about the facts?

Stop reacting to each other

When your partner behaves in a damaging way, your partner's behaviour does not give you the right to behave in damaging way too. You are responsible for your own reactions, and are not a reaction to your partner. If you are always a reaction to each other and not responsible for what you bring to your relationship, you will always be fighting.

Regardless of how your partner behaves, you always have a responsibility to keep it calm, gentle and respectful.

If you speak badly to your partner, you are both responsible for keeping it calm and trying harder. A relationship is not a game in which you try to trip up your partner for misbehaving – it is a team effort where the experience of your relationship is a shared responsibility.

Questions to ask yourself
- If I am really upset and feel like fighting back, how can I keep myself calm?
- If my partner is reactive, how can I keep my side clean and not become reactive as well?
- How can I be more responsible about my reactions?

Don't lean on each other's fences

When partners comment on each other, I often imagine a neighbour leaning on a fence, telling you how to do things – where to plant your plants, or how to mow your lawn. Can you imagine how that would make you feel? Leaning on each other's fences is a bad habit. It shows that you believe you know your partner better than they know themselves, and that you have given yourself the right to tell them who they are. This is not only damaging, but also irresponsible.

The sooner you get off each other's fences and stop blaming each other for what has gone wrong, the better. If you spend your time pointing fingers at each other, you are on the wrong path. Instead, being responsible for yourself means scrutinising your own behaviour first and keeping your side of the fence clean. No matter how your partner behaves, speak honestly, calmly and respectfully. In this way, you maintain your own integrity and show respect not only for your relationship, but for yourself.

Questions to ask about your relationship
- What, for you, does it mean to lean on each other's fences?
- In which ways do we lean on each other's fences?
- How does it feel to lean on each other's fences?
- If we feel that we are starting to point fingers and blame each other, what can we do to get out of the blame game?
- Instead of blaming each other, what really is my responsibility in a disagreement?

WHAT TO DO

The following processes have proven to work for most couples:

Prioritise your relationship

We all know that it is human to want to share our thoughts with others. So, in periods of unpleasant fighting, we take our thoughts to a place where they are welcomed. When we get tired of carrying our thoughts on our own, we start sharing them with a close friend or family member. The closer you start to feel to this friend, the further away you move from the person you love the most.

If you disagree or are upset, speak to each other first.

You prioritise your relationship by bringing your emotions and thoughts to each other. If you speak to a friend or family member, you need to accept that you should share whatever you discussed with your partner. If you do not, you empty out the experience of your relationship as you deepen the experience of your friendships. You feel more disconnected and start living increasingly separate lives, but feel closer to the friends and family with whom you do share. Speaking to your friends and family and not to each other when you are upset thins out the experience of your relationship. You rob your relationship of an opportunity for connection.

Often, you keep your thoughts and feelings to yourself for hours, days and, sometimes, months, because you don't feel safe or brave enough to speak. When you are hurt or upset, you withhold your love and affection. You become reactive and defensive, or passive and silent. This is one definition of unhappiness: waking up and going to sleep every day in that unpleasant tense atmosphere, and learning to live your lives in two separate, silent worlds. Two disconnected worlds.

Stop the silence and the constant fighting, and start speaking your minds. This is the first step to moving closer to each other. One of the main aims of a relationship is to stay connected. If you are not interested in being connected, you should rather be on your own.

Questions to ask about your relationship
- How do we prioritise our intimate relationship over all other relationships in our lives?

- Which commitment or promise can we make to each other about sharing information with people outside of our relationship?
- How can we make sure that we are always on the same page in our relationship?

Stop the escalation

Most couples fight about how they speak when they disagree and completely forget what they started fighting about in the first place. Often, when I ask couples what one of their fights was about, they have to think hard. But they can tell me in detail how their partners damaged their relationship. How they fought was much more upsetting than what they fought about.

A gentle conversation about a disagreement can escalate rapidly into a wildfire. You start talking about a particular topic, and soon you are shouting or walking away.

Escalation is at the heart of disconnection. The more you argue about the way you speak to each other, the further you move away from the topic. Like the ripples from a pebble thrown into a pond, the more you argue rather than share your thoughts on a topic, the further away you move from the topic and from the heart of your relationship.

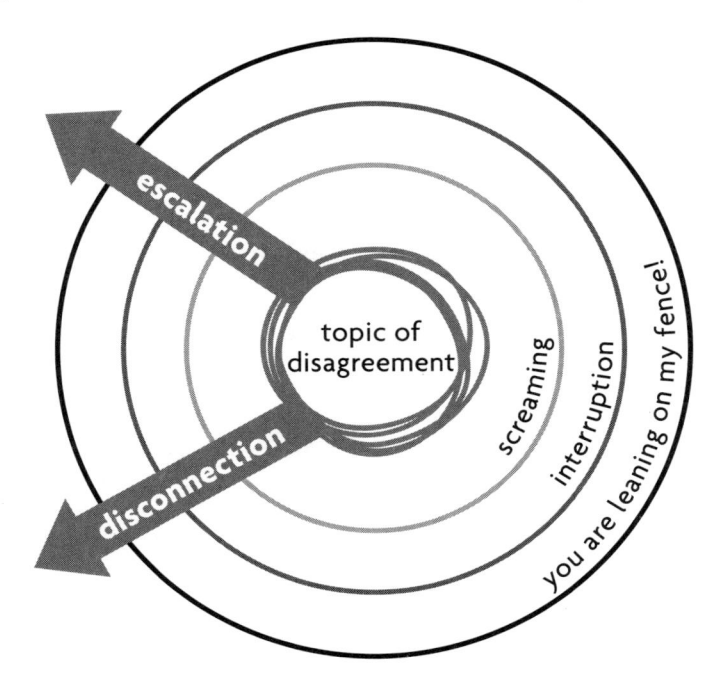

KNOW HOW TO DISAGREE

The intention of a good conversation is to pick up a topic or an upset and talk it through until you both feel understood. Your aim is to move from misunderstanding each other to reaching two or more points of understanding on the other side of the disagreement. So, the main aim of a conversation is to feel seen, heard and, above all, understood.

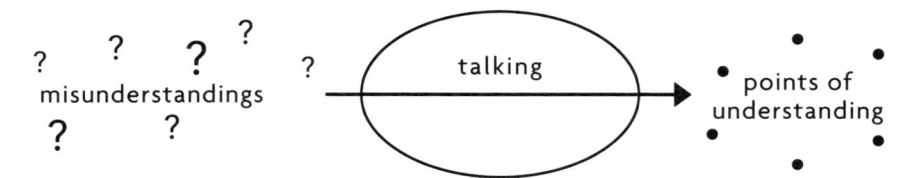

Move, through talking, from points of misunderstanding each other to points of understanding.

Questions to ask about your relationship
- When we start arguing about how we speak to each other instead of about the topic of our disagreement, how can we stop and get back to the topic?
- When we feel our conversation starting to escalate and get out of control, how can we calm down and start hearing each other again?
- How can we support each other in hearing our different points of view?

Share your upsets responsibly

If you partner upsets you, you are responsible for sharing your own upset.

Believing that your partner should know you well enough to see that you are upset and know what is wrong, is simply not reasonable. This belief, and the way in which you behave as a result of this belief, is not an act of love, but one of irresponsibility.

Instead of speaking about how upset or hurt we are, we tend to act out how we feel. We sulk, throw tantrums and refuse to participate, often becoming that child we used to be when we didn't get what we wanted in the shops.

If it bothers you, you must speak about it and not act it out.

Most couples tell me that they get upset when their partners cannot see that they are upset or do not try to approach them. But if you keep your thoughts to yourself, you are responsible for your own unhappiness as you did not speak up and give your partner a chance to rectify things. Your expectations are your unspoken needs and of no use if you do not express them. Maybe your expectations are hurting you and not your partner.

You are responsible for what you think and feel.

If we were all to take responsibility for what we feel when we feel it, the world would be a happier place. Expecting your partner to know your thoughts and feelings without conversation is expecting him or her to be a mind reader. Since most of us do not believe we are psychic, I suggest you claim responsibility for whatever you feel when you feel it and speak up about it as soon as possible.

If you get upset, you have a responsibility to speak up.

In simple terms, when you are upset, you need to say: 'I am really upset with you and would like to know when would be a good time to speak.' This is your invitation to talk.

Taking responsibility for your own thoughts and feelings does not mean that your partner has no effect on you. Your partner must accept that he or she has a very real impact on you. But your partner upsetting you does not give your permission to react. You are always responsible for what you feel and, more importantly, how you express it.

Questions to ask yourself
- When I am really upset, how can I share my feelings more responsibly in my relationship?
- When I am upset, how can I invite my partner into a conversation to share my upset?

Questions to ask about your relationship
- When we are upset, how can we indicate to each other that we need to talk?
- What is the best way to invite each other into a conversation?

Speak only for yourself

You do not live in your partner's body or mind, so it is best to not speak for him or her. When you speak, be mindful to speak only for yourself.

You are the expert about your own experience of life.

One way to speak for yourself is to replace sentences that start with 'you' with 'I' statements. So, instead of saying, 'You need to look at the way you are …', say, 'I would appreciate it if …' or, 'In my experience …' Speaking for your partner can misrepresent him or her, and is often the beginning of a fight.

Questions to ask yourself
- How can I remind myself to speak for myself, and not to start speaking for my partner?
- When we start speaking for each other, how can we bring ourselves back to speaking only for ourselves?

Never compromise

Compromise means finding the middle way between two very different opinions. For most, it means giving up what you need in a disagreement, to please your relationship. Giving up what really matters to you is often the beginning of resentment. For this reason, compromise does not bring happiness to a relationship.

Being upfront about what you really think and need seems much more important. Instead of compromising, focus on speaking your minds honestly and sticking to your two truths. Instead of giving up on what you know is true for you, see if you can accommodate both of your truths.

For example, suppose you need to buy a couch. You want the red couch, and your partner wants the blue couch. It is often not the best to compromise by purchasing the purple couch – neither of you will get what you prefer or need if you do. Rather keep looking at couches until you find the couch that neither of you can live without!

This is how couples make their most difficult decisions. Decisions that often lead to disagreement need to be talked about a lot more than decisions that don't. Keep speaking honestly and gently about what you think and feel, want and need, until you both start seeing more of each other's positions.

If you give in to a decision to please your partner and you wake up feeling resentful the next day or are constantly getting upset that you agreed when you wanted to disagree, rather be honest than keep your thoughts to yourself. Resentment is your cue that you have compromised and not spoken your truth.

What follows are the two most common questions that couples ask about making difficult decisions:

Question: What should we do if we agree to disagree, but still have to make a decision?

Answer: Important decisions need more discussion over time. If you both disagree, but have to make a decision in the end, you have to decide how important this is to you. Ask yourself, 'Is this decision part of who I am? By conceding this decision, would I be abandoning a part of my identity?' Disagreeing about smaller things, such as which couch to buy, is not as important, maybe, as disagreeing about choosing a school for your child. If it matters less to one partner than the other, then give over the decision. Doing so is like giving an emotional gift. If it does not define you, give it up, but make sure that giving this gift does not make you feel resentful, upset or compromised. If you do feel resentful, this decision is more important to you than you think, and you should not give up your position.

Compromise causes us to choose watered-down versions of what we really want. I strongly support knowing what you need or want, speaking your truths and standing strong. A person without opinions can be dangerous! Know what you are about and what you prefer. So, if you want the blue couch and your partner wants the red couch, and it matters to you both, do not buy either couch until you both see the one you like. Or, if you can afford it, consider taking turns to meet each other's needs: for example, this round I give to you, but next time my need is met.

Question: What do we do if we disagree, feel strongly about our two positions, and refuse to give in? For example, we have to agree on where our child will go to school?

Answer: Take more time to think and talk about the issue as much as you need to. Doubt means no! If you are not sure about a decision, the answer is still no, because doubt has never felt like a definite yes. It means do not make the decision hastily and think and talk as much as you need. When you have talked about it, slept on it and talked about it some more (without fighting!), the answer will become clear. The more time you spend on the decision, the clearer it will become. At the same time, some decisions on which you cannot agree can be deal-breakers. If a decision is important to you both, and no amount of dialogue results in agreement, it could mean that this relationship is not for you.

EMERGENCY RELATIONSHIP TOOLS

Like the handbrake in your car that you pull up in an emergency to prevent an accident, your relationship needs tools that you can use when things get out of control. Think about the biggest obstacles that stand in your way of hearing and understanding each other, and select the tools you need to remain respectful of each other in any situation.

The following tools can help you to change direction in your relationship's most difficult moments.

Put the topic on the shelf

When you don't like how your partner is speaking to you, or how they are behaving, or when you start losing control of your emotions, use the relationship skill of putting your upsets on the shelf or having a 'timeout'. In Chapter 2, you saw that when and where you have a conversation is one of the biggest influences on the conversation's success. When one partner feels like talking or sharing, it may not be the right time or place for the other, but when your partner tells you that, it can feel like you are being rejected. This may result in things getting out of control very quickly.

When you 'park' a conversation, your intention is not to avoid or ignore each other's experiences – it is to choose a time and place when you are both ready to talk. Using this tool is a way of taking care of your relationship.

If you struggle to do this, it is often best to remove yourself from the situation physically and leave the room. Allow each other to walk away on one condition: that you take the topic off the shelf within 24 to 48 hours. The one who walks away or calls the timeout is responsible for taking the topic off the shelf again when you are both ready.

Questions about your relationship
- What is our understanding of how we can use techniques such as putting topics on the shelf or timeout?
- What is the best way to put our out-of-control topics on the shelf?
- What is the best way for us to put a topic on the shelf that will not feel like rejection or avoidance?
- If we feel that our conversation is escalating and becoming damaging, what can we say to each other to stop the escalation?
- What can we say when our conversations get too much for one or both of us so that we don't upset our relationship?
- Which words or phrases should we avoid when we don't want to speak about something when it arises?
- How can we help our relationship by putting a topic on the shelf?

Talk about what you need

If you have tried your best to have a calm, honest conversation, but have struggled to speak respectfully and have started to fight, this tool can restore instant calm to your relationship.

Instead of fighting to be right, blaming each other for what is wrong and not hearing each other, change the topic – talk about what you need from each other.

Most disagreements and fights are about our not getting what we need. A relationship is about two people's needs and the happiness of your relationship will be determined by how often you play in each other's needs. Knowing and expressing what you need from each other steers your relationship in the direction of happiness.

Your needs should never be judged or questioned: if you need it, you need it and it should always be considered. So, if you are fighting or arguing, try to stop the conversation and ask each other, 'What do you need from me?'

```
        ┌─────────────────────────────────┐
       ╱                                   ╲
      │    ┌─────┐                ┌─────┐   │
      │    │ MY  │   BALANCE      │YOUR │   │
      │    │NEEDS│─────OF─────    │NEEDS│   │
      │    └─────┘                └─────┘   │
       ╲                                   ╱
        └─────────────────────────────────┘
```

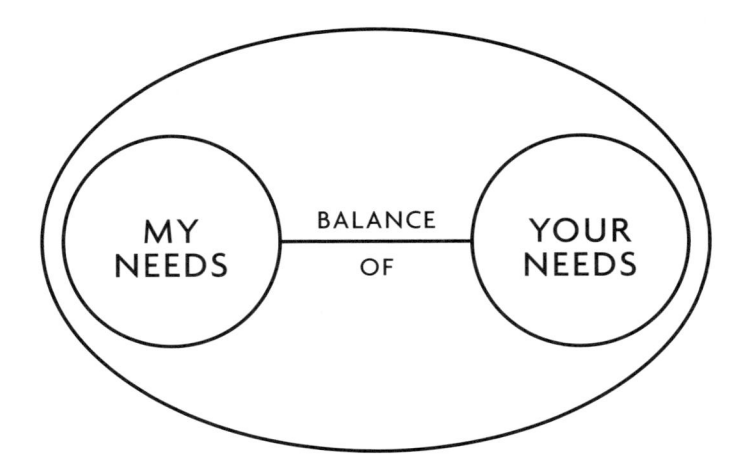

Your ability to meet each other's needs determines the happiness of your relationship. Balancing two people's needs in one space is happiness in action.

Extend an invitation to change

When you stop listening to and start screaming at each other, you can change the direction of your conversation by extending an invitation to change. If you are fighting about your different sets of needs, and refuse to listen or give each other what you need, extend an invitation to your partner to participate in meeting your needs. If your partner refuses to do so, invite him or her to change with you.

An invitation is a powerful way of asking your partner to make a change and be a part of what is important to you and your relationship. Invite your partner to:
- share;
- acknowledge your feelings or point of view;
- take responsibility;
- be gentler, kinder and more considerate;
- look and listen;
- come on a journey of change with you; and
- share in the joys of life.

Your invitations can be spoken, written or both. They are gentle invitations to support and be part of your relationship and each other.

They should feel neither patronising, prescriptive nor blaming, but honest and kind.

You will know best how to invite your partner onto a path of change. You may not always get a reply, but keep at it – every invitation creates an awareness of what you need in your relationship. Even if it is not acknowledged, it creates an opportunity to hear and see more of each other.

Questions to ask about your relationship
- Which kinds of invitations for change would we like to extend to improve our relationship?
- In the context of our relationship, what is the best way for us to communicate the need for change?

Speak to each other as if you are not alone

Couples often speak to each other in a much more controlled and respectful way in therapy than they do at home. The power of therapy often lies in the fact that another person is observing you. Being observed – witnessed – often reminds you to be more responsible with your words and actions. Over the years, I have asked couples to record their most difficult conversations. The second you press the record button on your phone, you start speaking to each other with greater respect.

EXERCISES FOR YOUR RELATIONSHIP

These exercises may help to keep your relationship in a respectful space:
- Think of a person you both know and respect. Imagine that this person is watching and listening to both of you during a conversation. Speak to each other as if this person is with you.
- Record your conversation if it gets out of control. Before the conversation, decide with who you might share this conversation. Of course, you will most likely not share it with anybody, but speak to each other as if you intend to do so.
- Listen to the recording of your conversation and make notes about what you could do differently.
- With your therapist's permission, record your difficult conversations and share them with him or her.

Find a good therapist

A good therapist can facilitate a change in your relationship and is often a last resort. You need to go for therapy if all your attempts to talk about an issue end in a fight. Constant fighting tells you that you are not seeing each other, and that you need skills to change and to deepen your understanding of your different experiences.

Find a therapist who specialises in relationships and who will give you new skills, direction and support. Often, change only happens after six to eight sessions of good therapy, but you need to keep going until you feel equipped to deal with your differences on your own. Therapy is only a temporary learning experience for a real-life relationship. You need to take your new skills home and apply them – to disagree, and see if you can handle it on your own.

IN CLOSING

These are the bad habits that you should avoid during a disagreement:
- interrupting each other;
- shouting (or any damaging behaviours);
- keeping your thoughts and feelings to yourself;
- fighting about the facts;
- reacting to each other;
- speaking for your partner; and
- leaning on your partner's fence.

The skills from which any relationship would benefit in a disagreement are:
- calming yourself down and gathering your thoughts before you speak;
- choosing your time and place carefully;
- accepting that people have different views;
- taking turns to speak;
- speaking about what upsets you and not acting it out;
- being genuinely interested in each other's different experiences;

- speaking only for yourself;
- taking as many turns as you need to reach an understanding;
- prioritising your relationship;
- preventing escalations;
- sharing your upsets responsibly;
- putting your upsets on the shelf if your conversation gets damaging;
- not compromising; and ...
- telling each other what you need.

Questions to ask about your relationship
- Of which areas and skills do we need to be mindful to improve the experience of our conversations?
- Where do we need to focus when we speak to each other? On which skills do we need to work harder?
- When we start to argue, what can we do to stop ourselves from doing more damage to our relationship?
- To which new ways of being in a conversation do we commit from this point to take better care of our relationship?
- How can we behave during a disagreement that will make us proud of ourselves?

AN EXERCISE FOR YOUR RELATIONSHIP
- Make a list of all the behaviours that neither of you want in your relationship any longer.
- List all the skills on which you need to work to improve your relationship experience.
- Set up a new agreement with terms for your relationship about how you promise to treat each other in the future.
- Make a promise to each other to try your best to treat each other with respect from this day onwards.

Chapter 4
a **break** in **trust**

You probably don't want to hear this, but if you have relationships, you trust is going be betrayed. Every person I have met has experienced some sort of break in trust; if you are lucky enough to have been spared this in the past, you will most likely experience it in the future. This is not necessarily negative or even a warning. As painful as it is, it could be one of your most life-changing experiences.

A break in trust is an important and, often, rich experience. A relationship that has experienced the pain of a break in trust has more depth than one that has not. It will teach you a lot about yourself and your relationships.

When life is uncertain and hard, it often gives you perspective about what matters. What is important?

A break in trust will show how committed you are. During the crisis, you will see the truths about your relationship. Are you really committed? Are you really loyal? Are your really responsible? Do you really care?

Even if you don't want to, you will learn more about yourself, your relationship and the world in the moments when you lose trust. It is the time to look beyond the pain and take note of what life is trying to say to you. Whereas there are many more pleasant ways of learning about life, a break in trust seems to be the ultimate schooling for most of us.

A break in trust ultimately affects who you think you are.

A break in trust will challenge not only the core of your relationships, but your own core too. It leads us to question many of our beliefs. It messes with our most important internal compass – the voice that guides us, also known as our intuition or gut feeling.

It forces us into that in-between space of questioning, a space in which you ask more questions than you answer:
- Can I trust him?
- Does she love me?
- What is he thinking?
- Is she telling the truth?
- Am I still attractive to him?
- Am I still enough?
- What do I need?
- Who am I?

For this reason, a break in trust is often followed by an experience of feeling lost, in limbo, confused, uncertain and disconnected.

A break in trust makes you question not only your partner and your relationship, but yourself above all.

Like a stone dropped into a pond, a break in trust has a ripple effect on almost every relationship in our lives. First, we question our partner and our relationship. Next, uncertainty creeps into our sense of self. Sometimes, it even changes our basic beliefs in life and human nature.

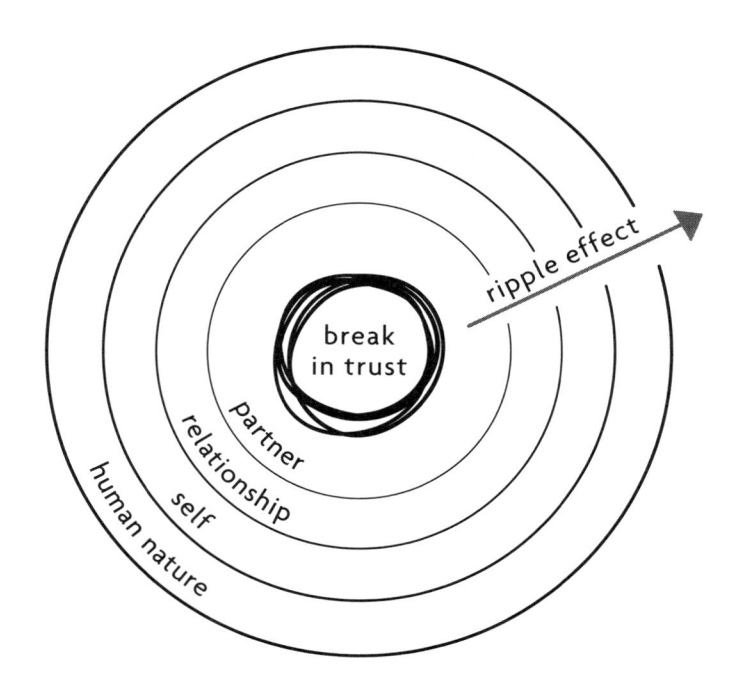

THE MEANING OF TRUST

It is important to think about what trust means and how it can be broken. It seems to happen easily, but receives little consideration.

Trust is about promises and agreements. It is about our agreements, expressed and silent, with the people with whom we are in relationships . The promises and agreements we think we have are the building blocks of how we experience what we call love. Betraying or breaking the agreements and promises we have made, calls the building blocks of our relationship into question. Love, respect and trust often come into question.

Trust is about knowing where you stand. To trust, you need to understand, and know where you stand with, each other. To stay connected, you need to know where you are emotionally, mentally, financially, morally, spiritually and physically. If you do not know where you stand with each other, life could surprise you and you might find yourself with an unexpected crisis.

Trust is when words are consistent with actions. The people you trust mean what they say and say what they mean. Their actions and words will be the same. Saying something but not acting it out creates the experience of distrust.

Trust is about feeling safe. You need to feel safe to be able to let go of the need to control each other and fall into a vulnerable space. To trust is to feel safe enough to be vulnerable. If you cannot be vulnerable, it is difficult to feel love. Love is vulnerable and soft and very gentle.

Questions to ask about your relationship
- What is the meaning of trust in our relationship?
- Which actions and behaviours create our experience of trust?

YOUR SACRED AGREEMENTS

Adult relationships are conditional. This does not mean that they are based on rules and regulations – it means that in any adult relationship, we have certain expectations, preferences and conditions that make us feel safe and loved. Not hurting me on purpose, being honest, and giving our relationship priority over others are some of the most common conditions for most adult relationships. These preferences or conditions are the terms of your 'love agreement'. They are sacred agreements as they protect and support the core experiences of your relationship: loyalty, trust, responsibility and respect. They are the actions of love.

The sacred agreements of most people's relationships only come to the fore on their wedding day and during a crisis. In other words, we think we have unconditional relationships until we hit a crisis in which one or both partners have broken the relationship's agreements.

Some of the sacred agreements for most relationships are:
- You will not lie.
- You will not cheat.
- You will not give priority to others over our relationship.
- You will treat me with respect.
- You will take care of me when needed.
- You will choose my side and be loyal to our relationship.
- You will love me.
- You will not judge me.
- You will not leave me.

All relationships have agreements and conditions. They are the building blocks of your relationship and are there to uphold your experience of love. Therefore, the idea that you will love me and accept me no matter what is simply not true. Unconditional love and acceptance are for children and animals. Because trust is made up of agreements, adult relationships are conditional.

The irony is that if you know what your relationship is built on and you stick to your agreements, you don't need to focus on the conditions and agreements. In a way, having a trusting relationship feels unconditional and doesn't feel bound by rules, conditions and regulations. Trusting relationships are grounded in the belief that you can both be who you are without the fear of getting hurt or being judged. They are healthy, honest, loving relationships, built on sacred agreements that give you the freedom to be who and what you are.

As soon as one partner abuses this freedom to be and breaks your agreements, however, you suddenly become aware of all of your relationship's agreements and conditions. Your relationship starts to feel more like a relationship of transactions and agreements than unconditional love and acceptance.

It is interesting how the person who asks for an unconditional adult relationship is often the one who breaks the relationship's rules or who is irresponsible. 'You need to accept me as I am' and 'This is me, take it or leave it' are statements that someone would make who does not want to respect your relationship's agreements. This person usually wants to do what he or she wants, when he or she wants to – which is why he or she asks for unconditional acceptance.

If you know your sacred agreements and if you treat them with respect, you give your relationship the gift of freedom.

Questions to ask about your relationship
- What are some of the obvious agreements in our relationship?
- Which agreements or expectations do we have when we talk to each other?

AN EXERCISE FOR YOUR RELATIONSHIP
- Write down and discuss the sacred agreements on which your relationship is built.
- What would we do if we broke our agreements?

WAYS TO BREAK TRUST

The most obvious break in trust is cheating: the promise that we will not have sex or share intimately with anyone but our partner. But this is not our first experience of a break in trust. Our first experience of a break in trust often involves our parents.

Our first wound

Our first and primary break in trust often happens in our relationships with one or both of our parents. Like any child in a relationship with their parents, we seem to have expectations of our parents that can last until the day they die. We may be adults having an adult relationship with our parents, but we still expect some mothering and fathering. Whereas we no longer need parenting, we load our relationships with our parents with our expectations of parenting.

We trust that our parents will mother us or father us, choose our sides, protect us and love us unconditionally. And when they don't, we are so hurt and upset by our own expectations that we call it our parents' 'lack of parenting'. We tell our friends 'shocking' stories about how our mothers hurt us or fathers ignored us, about how we didn't get the love we deserved.

You parents failing you inflicts your first, big emotional wound. We carry this wound from our parents into our adult relationships, playing it out in our friendships and intimate relationships. The most common emotional wounds are about being rejected, unloved, abandoned, ignored, neglected, not chosen – they are all about never feeling good enough or loved enough or seen enough.

Where your expectations of your parents originate is worth looking at. Often, we look to other families, or movies and books, for lessons about how our parents should have behaved. The dominant messages from our culture and society shape our expectations of our parents.

But maybe your expectations of parenting are not in line with your parents' expectations of parenting. Your parents may have "failed" you, but they did the best with what they had. Maybe your silent expectations or fantasies of the perfect parent are what is hurting you. This does not mean that your parents haven't hurt you – it simply means that your expectations of your parents may not be in line with their best or worst attempts at parenting.

Instead of carrying your expectations, it seems important to speak to your parents about your expectations. Share your expectations and preferences about, and needs for, parenting with them. It seems obvious that if you do not speak openly and honestly about what you expect in any relationship, you continue to hurt yourself with your own expectations. By sharing your expectations with your parents, you invite them into your needs. You give them a chance to listen, and to rise to the occasion or even make changes

An expectation is a silent, unexpressed need.

So, think about speaking up about what you need, rather than carrying so many silent expectations that hurt you. If you have told your mother or father more about what you need from them, and they have not been open to hearing or understanding you, you have a parent who is unable, unwilling or not ready to change for you. If you are blessed with a parent who is willing to hear you and accommodate your needs, you can step into a healthy adult-to-adult relationship.

The fantasy that fuels your expectations may be preventing you from seeing who and what your parents really are.

If your mother or father is not open or willing to change, it seems better to see them as honestly and accurately as possible. Step out of the fantasy of what you want them to be and see the reality of who they are. Who is your father, really? What is your mother really like? The more you look at them truthfully and honestly, despite the pain of doing so, the more your expectations fall away. You liberate yourself from untruths and fantasies of your parents and step into the truth about them. Who are they and what is our relationship really about?

Our parents will, most likely, be our primary wound and our biggest life lesson. Speak about your needs and desires in any relationship, or your needs will remain fantasies, hopes and dreams that can only disappoint you. Never build a relationship on silence – build it on truth. And the truth is that you can never build any relationship on a fantasy, but only on what you really – honestly have right now.

Our second break in trust

We enter into friendships and intimate relationships with expectations of love – I expect you to treat me kindly, love me as I am and never lie to me. People who were fortunate enough to miss the disappointment of their parents' first wound tend to get hurt in their first friendships or intimate relationships. And it seems that these experiences hurt and shape us forever.

In intimate relationships and friendships, the injuries are often about not being chosen. The primary experience is about rejection. This wound shapes us with a deep sensitivity to rejection. The need to be liked and accepted by others becomes so important that you sacrifice your needs to please others. To avoid the familiar pain of rejection, we sacrifice who we are.

The obvious betrayal of trust: the affair

Although there are many ways to break someone's trust, having an affair seems to be the ultimate betrayal. Even the words 'having an affair' are deceitful: it is not colourful or glamorous – it is a massive crisis!

An affair is a person and relationship in crisis.

An affair is loaded with layers of betrayal. It calls so many of the building blocks of your relationship into question – not only your trust that is in question, but also your desirability, attraction, loyalty and respect. The basic building blocks of love come into question, which is why an affair has such power and causes such pain.

The madness of an affair does so much damage to all of your relationships – especially to your relationship with yourself. In my experience, it is a very tough test for any relationship.

This is what I have learnt from listening to people who are trying to recover from the break in trust that an affair causes:
- The person causing the break in trust seldom thinks about the full consequences of the impact of the break in trust. In my experience, most consider only the superficial consequences of a betrayal. There are many reasons for being in denial or unaware of these

consequences, but the truth is that if you had really thought about the consequences of a break in trust for everyone involved, you may never have caused it in the first place.
- The person who caused the break in trust often forgives himself or herself long before the person on the receiving end of the betrayal has forgiven him or her. This means that the person who caused the betrayal often recovers more quickly, and wants to move on from the betrayal sooner.
- Most people who cheat on their partners are first offenders. They have no history of cheating, and overstepped the boundary just this once.
- A person with a history of proven infidelity may have a sex addiction or a serious problem speaking the truth. Of course, it is dangerous to make sweeping generalisations about human experiences, but I do know that if you have a history of cheating and lying, you will most likely continue to do so. The risk of the pattern of cheating or lying repeating itself seems higher for the serial cheater than the one-off offender.
- Sometimes, cheating or breaking an agreement can be a form of commentary about your relationship. It tells you something about your relationship that you might find difficult to hear. A break in trust is an opportunity for truth, and speaks of a need that has not been met for a long time in your relationship.
- Sometimes, a break in trust has very little to do with your relationship. It says lots more about the person who has broken the trust than it does about your relationship. It may be that your partner is showing a part of himself or herself that you might be struggling to see.
- You cannot sweep a betrayal of trust under the carpet. If you ignore it and move on as if nothing happened, you will never recover. The injury of the betrayal will resurface in your relationship until you give it proper attention.
- Knowing the details of the betrayal seems essential for the healing process. This is not always about knowing every little detail. Rather, it is about having the opportunity to ask the questions your need to ask to heal, and getting what feels like honest answers.

If you have betrayed your partner, your willingness to answer his or her questions about your betrayal and your honesty is your first contribution to restoring trust. In other words, how you participate in the process will show you signs of trust. The process of asking questions and getting honest answers is one of the most important processes on the road to recovery and healing.

- Being on the receiving end of a break in trust does not give you the licence to treat your partner 'badly'. Speaking to your partner in a damaging way creates a second layer of betrayal and makes the situation worse. Therefore, it is important to maintain respect during the recovery period.
- Women tend to betray their partners with someone they know, and men with someone they don't. Of course, this is not always the case.
- When women betray their partners' trust it is often about an unmet emotional need in their relationship. When men do so, their reasons are more a reflection of themselves than of their relationship.
- Trust is never broken in general terms. You lose trust in very specific areas of your relationship, so be careful to not generalise your experience. You may, for example, trust your partner financially or as a parent, but not in having boundaries with alcohol or saying no to friends.
- To recover from the betrayal of an affair, both partners need to do some work on themselves and their relationship. Even if you are not in any way responsible for the choice of betrayal, you still need to participate and make changes to recover fully.

I have never met a single person who thought fully about the consequences of his or her affair for himself or for the people around them. Except for the obvious loss of trust, an affair comes with multiple other losses – the loss of respect, friends, a close-knit family, financial losses and, above all, self-respect. The most common way of betraying your partner may be to shout at and verbally abuse him or her, yet an affair has so much more power than many other forms of betrayal. We all know that we are not supposed to speak to each other in damaging and hurtful ways. But somehow this agreement is easily broken without thinking about the real consequences for your relationship.

The every-day breaks in trust

Having an affair is not the only way to break the trust in your relationship. A break in trust in any relationship is a break of all the relationship's every-day agreements, which can be spoken (clearly communicated) or, often, unspoken. We assume that we are on the same page. We assume that we will not lie, keep secrets or give someone else priority. We expect that we, our life partners and friends will take care of each other by sticking to these every-day agreements. And we regard these agreements and how we honour them as signs of love and respect – 'If you love me, you will speak kindly to me.' If your partner does not stick to your agreements, he or she does not love or respect you.

But these agreements are easily broken:
'You promised me you would be home by 10pm.'
'You promised me you wouldn't speak to her.'
'Why did you tell my mother about our finances?'
'Why did you tell our friends about your new project at work before telling me?'

Maybe this is why we forgive the betrayals of our unspoken agreements more easily, yet really struggle to recover from the obvious betrayal of an affair. It seems even if we never speak about the possibility, this is the one agreement to which most assume we have a full commitment. It is in these every-day breaks of trust that you lose your love.

Reactions to a break in trust

When people get caught or their deceit comes to the surface, their first response to their lie is often another lie. People tend to deny the truth to protect themselves and, maybe, their partners. Therefore, for most the first line of response to deceit is more deceit in the form of a lie.

Other responses to a break in trust include:
- defensiveness;
- playing down the betrayal;
- denial;
- relief;
- connection and closeness;
- complete shock and surprise;
- blame; or …
- anger.

It is ironic that a break in trust and the honesty that follows it can often result in a period of closeness and connection, despite the fact that your relationship is in crisis. It reminds us about the truth that speaking honestly and openly can bring us closer together and make us feel more connected.

Why people break the agreements of their relationships

Sometimes, a break in trust points to something that is missing in your relationship. It can reflect your unmet needs. People break the agreements of their relationships when they are not getting what they need. When you are neither getting what you need from your relationship nor speaking about it you tend to gravitate towards what you need. But if your relationship is not giving you what you need, you are responsible for giving your relationship a chance by speaking honestly and openly about your needs. You cannot blame your relationship for your choices, but your relationship could be experiencing the following if a break in trust occurs:
- A loss of attraction to each other;
- A lack of real communication – the way in which you try to recover from the break in trust clearly reflects how you communicate and do not communicate in your relationship;
- A lack of emotion, connection and understanding;
- A lack of understanding of each other's needs – our basic human needs are to be touched, seen, loved, desired, prioritised and

acknowledged. If we express these needs and they are not met, we will seek what we need elsewhere. This is why it is important to stay connected to each other throughout your life;
- One person feeling alone or lonely in your relationship; or
- A relationship crisis (after being together for 10 to 15 years).

A break in trust is often not a reflection of your relationship. Often, we break our agreements because of a problem in our relationship with ourselves. In your relationship with yourself, you could be experiencing the following:
- A mid-life crisis if you are between 40 and 55;
- Depression, with infidelity as a 'mood lifter';
- Not taking care of yourself (self-neglect);
- The need to have your ego stroked (selfishness and narcissism);
- Insecurity (same thing, different language as ego);
- Curiosity;
- The habit of avoiding your real issues and sweeping problems under the carpet;
- A pattern of deceit and manipulation;
- A problem with speaking the truth – when you lie to yourself, you lie to your partner;
- An emotional pattern of avoidance;
- A loss of attraction to yourself;
- A lack of boundaries;
- Sexual dysfunction or sex addiction; or
- A drug or alcohol problem.

To recover from a break in trust, it is important to understand why you broke the agreements of your relationship. It seems important to look at yourself and understand what you need to work on to restore the trust in your relationship. Always remember that no reason justifies a break in trust.

THE TRAGEDY AND THE IRONY

The way in which you choose to recover from a break in trust is a direct reflection of your communication style, your conflict style and your commitment.

How well do you communicate?

How do you manage conflict?

How committed are you?

The irony is that, to recover, you now need to use an old way of speaking that didn't work for you before the break in trust. If you felt bullied in your relationship before, for example, you might feel even more bullied now. Often, the affair may become your sole focus, and not your past communication styles. But to recover from a break in trust, you need strong communication tools and to know how to disagree. If these were not part of your relationship before, your recovery will have to look beyond the affair and work on how to speak to each other in the presence of a crisis. This means that your recovery process is always about two people's contributions to a new direction, even if only one partner broke the trust.

Recovering from a break in trust requires change from both of you.

The way you in which you speak to each other in the recovery process can make or break your relationship. In other words, if you think a break in trust gives you the licence to treat each other with disrespect, you empty out what is left of your relationship. An affair can do a lot of damage, but how you speak about it can, sometimes, do even more. Discussing it disrespectfully is a second break in trust – when you do so, you both contribute to the crisis in your relationship.

Restoring trust is about slowly rebuilding the parts of your relationship that matter to you the most – putting back some trust, respect, honesty, loyalty, attraction and commitment. Even if you are not the one who broke the trust, you have to accept that you need to participate in the process to save your relationship.

A break in trust is a moment of truth.

When your agreements are broken, you feel so hurt and shocked that you no longer see your promises to each other in the same way. But the moment your trust gets broken you step into the truth – you see your partner, mother, father or friend for who he or she is. In this moment of truth, you both clearly see what the building blocks of your relationship are. As upsetting as this can be, it is a moment of truth in which you can speak about what you really think your relationship is made of.

A crisis is an opportunity to speak the truth.

Even if you know this is true, it can be difficult to make sense of it all when your trust is broken to move beyond the emotion and learn some lessons. Determine what this moment in time is telling you. You might learn something about your partner's real feelings or personality that you would never have learnt otherwise – that he or she can be impulsive, selfish or inconsiderate.

If your partner has broken your heart because he or she has broken your trust, you can take steps to restore trust in your relationship. Whether he lied to you, she didn't consider you in a decision, or he didn't stand up for you, you can trust again. As damaging as a break in trust can be, and as much as it can destroy the building blocks of your relationship, the truth is that trust can be rebuilt.

HOW TO RESTORE TRUST ON YOUR OWN

To restore trust in a relationship, you need two people to participate in the process of restoration. In therapy, I often see only one partner trying desperately to feel safe and trust again.

If someone has broken your trust, and you alone are willing to restore it, consider any of the following steps to free your life from distrust:

Adjust your expectations

When people in therapy complain about their partners, mothers, fathers or friends, I say, 'I don't see you mother sitting next to you. She is not in therapy. I'm not seeing her making any changes.' All I am trying to say is that change lies with you, and not with the person who is not in the room. Only you can make the changes you need to make. If you don't like the things your mother does, for example, the best thing you can do is to see an accurate picture of her and adjust your expectations accordingly. If your partner gets mean when she is not getting what she wants, or if he expresses himself awkwardly, the best you can do is see as much as you can with honesty, and with some compassion and some love.

Check your agreements

If you feel upset because of a broken agreement, whether spoken or unspoken, revisit your agreements – or, even better, make sure you are in agreement. This involves a simple conversation in which you make a list of all the agreements that you think your relationship has. It can be good to write them down, as a constant reminder of the promises that your relationship holds.

Questions that might guide you during this conversation:
- What are the vows, promises, terms, rules or agreements that your relationship entails?
- Which agreements do you have about trust?

Set some boundaries

If you don't like the way people treat you, you alone can change it. Nobody treats you badly, until you allow them to. If you don't like what you are getting, you have choices: leave, say no, or say something.

Put an end to the fantasy: speak the truth

A very important step is to stop building your relationship on what you would like to have, and start building it on what you do have – right here, right now. You may have found yourself caught up in a fantasy of what is possible based on small glimmers of hope or good memories, instead of focusing on what you are getting in reality. This comes from many deep-seated subconscious beliefs, such as change is always possible and, if you treat someone well, they will treat you well in return. It comes from the belief that what you give, you will get.

It is a misguided understanding of a belief in karma: if you think that giving more will, one day, reward you with the same love, respect and generosity that you wish for, you are mistaken and may be deceiving yourself. Giving without getting what you need is often called being used and abused.

You will only get what you give if both of you are generous, kind and loving. If your partner takes more than he or she receives, you will feel cheated, resentful, unloved and misunderstood. Do not be ambitious about this by trying to give more to get more. Focus, rather, on speaking the truth and giving to those who give.

You will only get what you give if both of you are giving.

The question is, 'What am I really getting from this relationship?' Connecting with the truth about what you are really getting can be liberating and hurtful at the same time.

Take a new position silently and strongly

Decide if this relationship is really taking care of you. If it is not, change your position. If speaking about your decision to step away from the relationship will not make any real difference to the relationship, change your position silently. This means that to take better care of yourself, you will distance yourself from, or end, the relationship. If you want to give the relationship another chance, speak about the changes in your relationship before you put them into action. This may give the relationship a chance to change.

If you have expressed your needs and the relationship is still resisting change, you still have the power to make a change. It takes two people to change a relationship. If you are still not getting enough of what you need, and you have expressed your needs over time, take care of yourself by ending the relationship.

HOW TO RESTORE TRUST WITH YOUR PARTNER

If you are lucky enough to have a partner who is willing to work on restoring the trust in your relationship with you, any of the following steps might assist you along the way.

Have lots of honest conversations

Have honest conversations about what you want and need, even if doing so is hurtful. How you speak to each other shows each other how committed you really are to the process of restoring each other's trust. The way in which you speak to each other also shows how much respect for each other is left in the relationship. In therapy, the person whose trust has been broken often needs to speak more. But I have learnt that listening to the person who broke the trust is often more healing.

Reach a clear, complete understanding of why it happened

You need to make sense of something you thought your partner would never do to you. You cannot walk away from this crisis without a clear, in-depth understanding of why you or your partner risked your relationship and family for a secret. Superficial explanations like 'I was insecure' or 'I don't know why I did it and I'm really sorry' are not going to cut it. Tell your partner how you make sense of your own behaviour.

Once you and your partner have made sense of what has happened, a **real apology** will follow – not a shallow 'I'm sorry', but an in-depth, self-aware explanation of your own understanding of your own behaviour. There is safety and calm in making sense of why your partner broke your trust.

Patience with the person on the receiving end of the break in trust, and with the partner who has broken your trust, is very important. You will both need to be very gentle and patient. Being patient with your partner's hurt and anger means not attacking back, not meeting anger with anger. It means staying calm about and being gentle with his or her emotions.

Show willingness to be open about any aspect of the truth

Trust is about knowing where you stand. One way of getting there is to ask all of your questions.

Couples often bring a list of questions to therapy. The partner who has been hurt feels that he or she failed to get the answers to these questions at home, and that detailed answers to every question will make him or her feel better. I find that a willingness to participate in the process of answering questions is even more important than the answers themselves. The answers can bring relief, but how hard the offender tries to please his or her hurt partner in this process is one of the most important steps in restoring trust.

The offending partner may feel that answering the questions will damage the relationship further, and refuse to participate in the process as a result. It is, of course, his or her right to say no, but doing so often becomes a source of further hurt. Unwillingness to participate is often seen as another example of the lack of respect, adding to the experience of distrust.

It is difficult to hear that another person made your partner laugh when you did not, for example. Yet, hearing it seems essential. It is better to know the real reasons for what happened – the truth – than not to know. Without the truth, you cannot let go of a hurtful experience.

I am often reminded about the following important truths:

- What is important to one partner but not to the other should be taken seriously – if it matters to one partner, it should surely matter to the relationship.
- A willingness to try, or to participate in, something that does not matter to you, but which matters very much to your partner, is an act of respect and love. Your willingness is at the heart of trust.
- If you do not speak the truth when you have lied, you may never fully heal and will likely keep circling back to that space of unanswered questions.

- Not knowing what really happened becomes an empty, nagging space that we fill with more questions than answers – questions about our relationship but, above all, about ourselves. We question ourselves when we don't know where we stand. A relationship that makes you question yourself is, or has likely been, damaging to your sense of self.

Never call your partner overly sensitive or emotional

Saying things like, 'Maybe you are just being oversensitive' trivialises and disregards you partner's feelings – feelings that you have most likely caused!

Sit with both parties' emotions in a calm and kind way

This is often difficult. The fact that you are shocked, hurt and broken does not give you the right to abuse your partner with your emotions. One partner breaking the agreements of your relationship can tacitly permit the other partner to start doing so as well – for example, by speaking to you disrespectfully.

We are all responsible for maintaining respect in how we speak to each other. It is important for both parties to keep it as gentle, calm and honest as possible. Being hurt does not give you permission to add destruction to your relationship.

Offer constant affirmations and reassurances

Constant and never-ending reassurances are essential. The offender needs to say 'I love you' and 'I want to be with you' constantly. If the offender fights this, he or she has not yet learnt to take responsibility for what he or she has done. If you have betrayed your partner with someone else, it is obvious that your partner needs to be told that you want to be with him or her.

Affirmations and reassurances must be constant and repetitive. A one-off reassurance is not enough. Reassure your partner every time it is needed and remember that your best reassurance is only as good as your last one.

Show affection

Touching and holding each other is a non-verbal acknowledgement that you see each other, and that you may be really sorry.

Have complete transparency about the tools used for the deceit

If you used you phone or laptop as a tool for breaking the trust in your relationship, consider trying a period of complete transparency about this tool. This means having full access to each other's technology at all times for a set period – for three months to a year, for example. During that time, all tablets, mobile phones, laptops and other screens are free for both partners to view, at any time – no more secret access codes or second e-mail addresses.

Couples who refuse to participate in this step often struggle to get past this point. I feel that this is necessary, even if it compromises your private space. The sooner you show willingness to participate in the process, and implement it, the sooner the need for it will go away. Most people cheat on their partners through the use of technology; computers and phones are an easy pathway to a secret world.

Show some appreciation

If your partner is fighting for the relationship, or you can see that he or she is really trying to restore your trust, it is important to acknowledge what you see and show some appreciation and gratitude for his or her efforts. Thanking each other for working on your relationship, acknowledging your partner's attempts and expressing gratitude can accelerate the healing process.

Relinquish control

Trust is about letting go of your need for control. Your trying to control every aspect of your partner's behaviour could leave you exhausted and undermine your trust over time. The belief that controlling your partner will make you feel more secure in your relationship is not true. Trying to control another person's thoughts and actions is impossible and exhausting.

If your partner has tried their best to answer your questions and show their commitment, let go of your need to control the outcome of this process. Focus, instead, on accepting each other's attempts as truthful. Managing your partner's commitments and agreements and the boundaries of your relationship will not make you feel safer and more trusting. It is an exhausting and controlling process that will never give you the outcome you seek. Even if doing so resulted in the commitment or behaviour you wanted, if the outcome originated from your control, and not from your partner's own responsibility, it will likely feel like a hollow victory. Relinquish control; invite each other to take responsibility and speak the truth. Therein lies your peace.

We often meet the insecurity that a break in trust causes with a need for control, and express this insecurity as anger, as doing so feels more empowering. But remember that your expressions of anger could cause a second break in trust.

Forgiveness is about speaking the truth and making sense of what has happened – it is about finding meaning. Understanding that your partner is human, and developing a deep emotional understanding of why the break in trust happened, can really support you in letting go of an experience. This is what it means to have compassion. Putting your experience aside and really trying to understand another's experience in depth can create a feeling of compassion.

Being willing to give it your all to restore trust – trying your best to make up for what you have done – is the best you can do to restore trust. It speaks of real remorse and is an affirmation that the partner who broke your trust is now fighting for you. Who wouldn't need to feel this in that moment of insecurity?

It is not easy for both parties to be that honest and open about their thoughts and feelings, but they have to push through and learn new ways of speaking to and being with each other.

THE TRUSTING RELATIONSHIP

The following actions give any relationship the experience of trust:

Know where you stand with each other

Staying connected to the experiences in your lives through sharing gives you a good sense of where you are in your relationship. If, at any point, someone were to ask you where you are and where your partner is in life, you should have some sense of what is going on. Knowing where you stand with each other on many levels is a safe and healthy place to be.

Behave consistently over time

Consistency does not mean that life is boring or predictable. It simply means that, because both of you take care of yourselves and your relationship, you do not experience extreme ups and downs. Your core remains the same over time, no matter how you feel.

Stay committed to change

A relationship that is committed to change has a strong chance of survival. When we make mistakes and hurt each other, we share a commitment to working on being better. Staying committed to change is an act of love and one of your most important contributions to trust.

Focus on the place where words and actions meet

Look beyond the promises that things will change in the future. Constant promises that are never kept are empty fantasies. More important than promises are actions and behaviours. Look at what your partner is doing now, rather than listening to what he or she is saying. Actions and behaviours tell you the truth, not promises and words. A healthy, happy relationship matches words to actions.

Treat each other with respect

Couples who treat each other with respect, even if they are hurt or lost, are taking care of their relationship. Treating each other with respect is your constant contribution to growing trust.

IN CLOSING

A new relationship with new commitments

After a big break in trust, you could feel as if you are entering into a completely new relationship or have new rules of engagement.

Trust can be restored at least once. But if you break the same promise a second or third time – if you break the agreement you promised you would not break again – then the path to recovery is rocky and lengthy.

If you are lucky enough to get a second or third chance, you will hopefully have learnt something and will not repeat the pattern.

After a break in trust, you often enter what feels likes a brand-new relationship. Couples tell me that how they speak, disagree, make love and enjoy life feels different after a break in trust. It seems important to keep working on the pain that a break in trust can cause. Carrying this pain for too long and too intensely brings it back into you relationship in the form of anger and resentment. The truth – that you are responsible for the pain you feel, even if your partner caused it – is one of the most difficult, but important, realities you have to face. Take charge of your feelings and speak to someone who can help you to let go of the anger and pain.

It is unrealistic to expect not to feel pain in the future. Honest healing is about making sense of what happened as much as possible, developing a deeper understanding of the what and the why, and forgiving yourself and your partner for what you allowed to happen.

Take back your perceptions

A break in trust can damage your perceptions of your partner and your relationship. Once you have taken steps to restore your trust, you also need to take back these perceptions. Reinstate what you believed to be true about each other and your relationship.

Renew your vows

After a break in trust, couples often renew their vows in front of family and friends or in private. This symbolises the lessons they have learnt in the process and their commitment to the future. It can also be restorative for the friends and family who supported you through a difficult time.

Questions to ask about your relationship
- Which steps can we take that will help us to feel a greater sense of trust in our relationship?
- Why are these steps important to us?
- How would these steps help us to restore our trust?

Chapter 5

sex and intimacy

If you feel sexually and intimately disconnected from your partner or yourself, or if your relationship is not satisfying you sexually – through a lack of sexual activity, enjoyment or pleasure – then this chapter is for you.

Sex and intimacy are pathways to closeness and connection, to yourself and to your partner. Like learning to have an honest conversation and to disagree with respect, having regular healthy intimacy and sex can move you in the direction of closeness. Sex and intimacy are powerful conversations, and one of a few pathways to closeness and connection to yourself and your partner.

Intimacy and sex are our reminders that verbal conversations are not the only way of connecting. I find that non-verbal behaviours are as important as verbal ones, with regular sex and intimacy being among the most powerful ways for you to 'speak' to each other.

UNDERSTANDINGS OF SEX AND INTIMACY

Your definition and understanding of sex and intimacy – their meaning for you – determine how you behave sexually and intimately, and are a good start if you want to make some changes to this part of your life. Ask yourself:
- What is the meaning of sex for me?
- What is the meaning of intimacy for me?
- How do sex and intimacy work, or not work, together for me?

Sex

My conversations with couples and individuals about their sex and intimate lives have made me realise that sex is difficult to define. Sex carries different meanings at different times in your life.

If you are honest with yourself about what sex means to you, you might find that sex is mainly about **attraction, physical connection, enjoyment and fun.** For you, closeness is not necessarily a prerequisite for great, satisfying sex. Having great sexual experiences, in which attraction and enjoyment are the aim, is more important than being intimately connected. At the same time, you will recognise that having a great physical connection and great sexual experiences with the same person over time will bring you closer intimately. Sex can move you from disconnection to connection, even if it is not your intention to become intimately connected. As your sexual connection grows, your basic human instinct for closeness may also grow. Although sex, for you, is more about a mutual physical understanding than an emotional one, you might become aware that enjoyable sex can strengthen your intimate and emotional connection.

For you, the energy of sex is intentional. It moves in the direction of your own intentions and that of your partner's desires, wants and needs. Sex is more about being physically desired and seen. When we feel seen on any level, we start connecting, even if connection was not our main intention. It starts – mainly – with being physically seen. The truth is that being seen physically can often create the experience of being emotionally understood. Therefore, even if you try to separate sex as a physical act from your emotions, enjoyable sex can be the beginning of an emotional and intimate connection.

Sometimes sex is selfish – more about satisfying your needs than your partner's. This might be difficult to admit. For some, sex is about physical pleasure and release, primarily your own. Your sexual partner getting some joy out of it may not have been your intention. But, separating your pleasure from that of your lover may not always be as satisfying for both parties. If sex is about physical pleasure and release for you, you may not need to be intimately or even physically connected to have sex. If this is how sex works for you, your mind and body might be in state of disconnection: you do not switch your mind or emotions on during sex, and view it as a primarily physical act.

Even if sex is more physical than emotional for you, it seems that sex does have deep-seated emotional effects that even the mind with the least awareness cannot deny. Your human need to be seen emotionally, and not only sexually, might surface over time.

For many, however, sex is about being understood both physically and emotionally, and it seems important to feel intimately connected to be sexually close. For you, sex is all about connecting your minds and your bodies. It is as important to know what you want, need and desire as it is to understand your partner's desires.

Sex and intimacy may grow together, over time. At times, you may feel a deep intimate connection; intense sexual satisfaction may characterise other times. Your ever-changing need for sex and intimacy depends on what is happening to your body, mind and soul in the different periods of your life. But sex and intimacy will always move up and down with you on the scale of your life. The sex you have now may even get better over the years, and your intimate connection will expand if you remain sexually connected.

Perhaps intimacy is a prerequisite for sex, for you. In other words, you need to know me physically and emotionally to have sex with me. But you do not think that an increase in intimacy will lead to more or better sex.

The energy of sex is primal. Sex is a straightforward, to-the-point conversation about what your mind and body desire.

Whatever the meaning of sex for you, sex is one of the **most honest** conversations you can have with your sexual partner and yourself. Being aware of your needs, what attracts you, and what you desire and enjoy in yourself and your partner is a gift to your relationship. It requires an awareness of your body's moods and desires, and of those of your partner – an awareness that should be shared, embraced and encouraged. Like a good conversation, what you say with honesty should never be judged. Sex is your free, open, non-judgmental space that requires you to know yourself and your partner in intimate detail. It is an adventure and a discovery. Like your ability to talk to each other, it should grow and improve as you do.

Sex is the ultimate freedom of expression. If your culture, gender, or community does not encourage you to know what you want or to have a voice, you may struggle to connect sexually with yourself and your partner. Your sexual growth may start with learning about what you really want, and not being who you think you are supposed to be or doing what you think you are supposed to do.

The best mindset for great sex seems to be a non-judgmental one that cannot be captured in the conventions and expectations of others. It is not about others: it is about knowing yourself and your partners in intimate detail. Knowing what you need, want or prefer is often labelled as 'selfish', but sex can only work if it is 'selfish'. I know what I like and you know what you want, and if what we need and want is a match, we can satisfy each other.

Intimacy

Intimacy is about sharing, closeness and touching. Speaking openly and honestly can increase the intimacy of your experiences. Touching and being touched, and kissing, hugging and stroking each other can create the closeness we call intimacy. Intimacy is verbal and non-verbal. It is about the small considerations, acknowledgements and affirmations.

The energy of intimacy is emotional. It is all about physical and emotional acknowledgement and being seen. It sends many messages, like: I want you, I love you, I desire you, I long for you. Every touch and every little word, sends the message that you see each other.

Intimacy does not lie easily. Faking an orgasm is easier than faking the passion or intention of an intimate connection over time. Even if you do try to fake enjoyment, you partner is likely to know whether your enjoyment came from a real place. The truth is in the eyes. Because intimacy seldom lies, your intimate life will reveal the truths about your relationship and yourself. In other words, how you behave intimately says something about who you are, how you think and where you stand in your relationship.

The complex relationship between sex and intimacy

The path to greater intimacy and the path to better sex are often not the same. The experience or energy of intimacy is not the same as the energy of sex. Intimacy is about feeling closer through touch and talking. The more you touch and the more honestly you share, the more intimate you get.

Intimacy can lead to more and better sex, but does not necessarily do so. Many couples feel very closely connected and have high levels of intimacy, but they do not want to have sex with each other. So, although intimacy can feel like the softer, more comforting side of sex, it is not necessarily the path to a better sex life. Intimacy does not lead to more or better sex.

Intimacy is about sharing and sex is about knowing what you want.

Knowing yourself and your partner is the path to better sex. Sex is about knowing what you need and want physically and expressing it with your body. It requires a connection with and understanding of your body and your mind. It reflects your understanding of your physical and emotional self.

To have great sex, it seems important to know your mind and body well. The more you know about how your mind thinks sexually and the better you know the pathways of your body, the better your sexual experience. Like your emotional self, your sexual self will grow in time. Most people come to know more clearly what they like and desire, and have less tolerance for what no longer works.

The truth is that sex and intimacy are among the most healing things that you can give your relationship. As one of the most important pathways to remaining close and connected, it is important to work at keeping them present in your relationship.

WHERE TO START
Change starts with a conversation

The truth is that a change in your intimate or sex life needs to start with a conversation. Many couples avoid speaking about their sexual and intimate lives. It is one of the most neglected conversation topics in most relationships, along with conversations about your emotional lives. In therapy, it is often last on the list of topics to discuss.

I often wonder why we are so afraid to speak about what we need from sex. The obvious answer is that sex is a sensitive issue, fraught with taboos and connotations. It is woven into religious and gender roles, and generations of men and women have received the message that talking about sex is not allowed. I often hear about the beliefs that may prevent us from talking openly about sex: sex is 'bad', so, as children, we are encouraged to avoid this 'inappropriate' topic.

If your sex life leaves you with more questions than answers, it might need some work. Many couples do not know where to start looking for the answers; sex and intimacy are full of unknowns for many. When they feel sexually or intimately disconnected, they often do not know how to fix things. Ironically, fixing your sex life often starts with an intimate conversation, not with a focus on sex.

It is as important to speak honestly about your sexual and intimate needs, desires and wants as it is to share your emotions in your relationship. Learning to let go of your blockages and talking openly and honestly about your sexual and intimate needs is the beginning of the change in your relationship.

Avoiding talking about your sex life means avoiding your relationship, a source of a lot of unhappiness for many couples. Silence has never made anyone happy. Your unspoken thoughts and feelings stand between you when it comes to your sexual connection. Not expressing what you think and feel creates a distance that also disconnects you sexually. So, starting to speak the truth about your sex life seems to be a very important first step.

If you are not sure what to talk about to reconnect intimately or sexually, start a conversation with any of the following questions.

What are my thoughts about sex and intimacy?
- Are we really designed to have regular, satisfying sex?
- Does our environment encourage a high level of sexual and intimate connection?
- Which beliefs do we carry about sex and intimacy? How do they affect us and our relationship?

Sex and intimacy are loaded with beliefs that directly influence and limit our levels of satisfaction and enjoyment in our relationships. For example, many couples believe that healthy relationships have regular, satisfying sex, and that if you are not, your relationship may be in trouble. Even if it is true, the belief that you need to have regular, satisfying sex puts a lot of pressure on many couples to perform from a disconnected space. Pressure, intimacy and sexual performance do not sit well in the same room. So, receiving this message about sex without a clear solution can create the kind of obstacles we feel in our sex lives.

We receive strong messages about frequency: if you don't have sex at least once or twice a week, your relationship is in trouble. We think that if our partners are not initiating sex with us regularly, they are losing interest in us – that we are no longer desirable or loved. But is this true?

The belief that being connected emotionally and intimately but not having regular, satisfying sex means that you are in trouble feeds our perfectionist, overachieving minds with high-performance expectations. Sex and intimacy are not about performance – they are about connection, enjoyment and fun.

We receive limiting messages about what defines sex: that penetrative sex is the only sex that counts. As a result, we miss out on hundreds of other very satisfying sexual and intimate behaviours and activities. This limits your sexual menu and creates sexual boredom.

We receive messages about satisfaction: that sex should always be extremely satisfying, stimulating and exciting. This creates so much performance anxiety that stage fright is not surprising.

For most people, the belief that the more intimately you are connected, the more sex you will have, is untrue. We believe we need to be intimately connected to enjoy sex. Many couples, however, enjoy high levels of affection and intimacy, but do not necessarily want to have sex with each other. The opposite is also true: some couples have great sex, but don't feel intimately bonded.

To add insult to injury, long-standing and new ideas about sex and intimacy surround us, affecting our own ratings of our performance. We should be open to sexual freedom, expression and exploration. We should be willing to explore, yet careful to avoid sexual injury. Maybe it is more about knowing yourself and where your boundaries are than about being open-minded or narrow-minded.

Look closely at your beliefs about sex and intimacy, as they can influence your sexual and intimate experiences. Our thoughts about sex and intimacy measure the success of our relationships. Often, our beliefs are simply not true, yet they dominate our sex and intimate lives. We hold onto these beliefs with fear and anxiety about losing our partners. The truth is that these beliefs could get you into trouble.

Questions to ask about your relationship
- What are some of our dominant beliefs about sex and intimacy?
- Where do our beliefs about sex and intimacy come from?
- What are these beliefs really doing to our experience of sex and intimacy?

What more would I like to experience with you, and what more do I need, sexually?

Instead of speaking about the problems with your sex life, steer the conversation in the direction of your needs, wants and preferences. This conversation may require some of the skills covered in earlier chapters (how to have a constructive conversation and how to disagree). Take turns, without interrupting, to talk about what more you would like to experience in your sex life. As always, both of your sets of needs are equally important. Instead of taking what you hear personally and reacting to it, listen with gratitude to what your partner is saying.

The happiness of your relationship is about balancing two people's needs. Similarly, how happy your intimate and sex life is is also about both of your sets of needs living happily in one space. If one partner's needs are valued more than another's, a relationship can feel like an unhappy place.

In practical terms, make one list containing the sexual needs of both of you, and see all of those needs as the basis of the work you need to do on your relationship in the future. This could, perhaps, become a new intimate challenge or an exciting sexual adventure. Your list of sexual needs points your relationship in new directions.

If your feel that one of your partner's needs or desires conflicts with your identity, speak about it and try to understand why you feel that way, and then take it off the list. Choose at least one or two of each of your needs and make suggestions for how you can accommodate them in the future. You are responsible for meeting your needs, and this means that you need to initiate and create the experience for your relationship. Of course, you both have to participate happily in each other's needs to get more of what you want.

Questions to ask about your relationship
- What more would I like to experience with you sexually?
- What more do I need in terms of intimacy?

I find that talking about your intimate needs is often a separate conversation, as the energies of sex and intimacy can be so different. For that conversation, however, apply the same process as you did when you talked about your sexual needs.

How are we programmed differently?

Without generalising about men and women's experiences, I have found that the different genders often have very different ideas about how to reconnect sexually or intimately and move beyond being sexually 'stuck'. So, speaking about your differences may be an eye-opener and give your relationship some direction.

The question I ask men and women is: 'What do you propose as your next step to feeling closer sexually and intimately?' In response, women often speak about their need for more intimacy to warm up sexually, and men often speak about sex as the path to greater intimacy. In other words, in my experience women often speak about being emotionally seen and understood as a prerequisite for sexual connection, whereas men seek sex as a pathway and solution of getting to a place of emotional connection. This, of course, is not true of all men and women, but does seem to hold for most relationships. It highlights men and women's different expectations of how to get sexually close – a difference that may explain why you feel 'stuck' sexually.

Because of these expectations, the process of sexual reconnection starts from two very different places, often causing sexual tension and further disconnection: men see having sex as a solution to sexual disconnection, whereas women feel the need to be seen before being touched. How can you touch me or make love to me if you don't even understand what I feel and think? First you need to see me before you can touch me; or, only if we touch or make love will we 'see' each other again. Both approaches are pathways to connection. They are equally important as connection is their main intention.

As you would during a constructive conversation, it is important to be mindful that what matters to one should matter to you both, as it always matters to the relationship. If your partner needs be to better understood first to connect sexually, then that is important and relevant to your relationship.

Questions to ask about your relationship
▸ When we feel sexually disconnected, what is the pathway to reconnection for me?
▸ What can we do for each other to reconnect sexually and intimately?

How is my sexual history affecting our relationship?
Your sexual history is relevant to your current intimate and sex life. Sexual or intimate injuries, such as childhood sexual abuse, play out in your sex life. Sexual abuse is a violation of your personal boundaries that can disrupt your ability to draw clear sexual boundaries. It can teach you to abandon your body and mind during sexual or intimate exchanges.

A history of sex, drugs and rock 'n roll may have created a similar sexual pattern that can challenge your ability to be present during sex and intimacy. Substances can cause an abandonment of yourself that can change your patterns of sexual pleasure. They often cause a loss of intimacy over time. If you have a history of sex on drugs, you may have difficulties connecting during intimacy and sex.

If you have had abusive, traumatic or invasive sexual experiences, you may experience a disconnection between your mind and body. What your mind says to you during sex and intimacy and how your body responds may not give you the same message. You need to examine and understand fear, blockages, resistance and a lack of openness to have a satisfying, connected sex life. A facilitated conversation, such as in a therapy context, is often useful. Understanding and awareness of how your history has shaped your experience of sex and intimacy can often dissolve sexual blockages.

Questions to consider
- How have the sexual experiences of my past shaped my sexual behaviour?
- How is my sexual history affecting our relationship?

How do sex and power work in our relationship?

Your sex life reflects what is happening and has happened in the life of your relationships, past and present. Sex, for most, is a conversation of very few words. If your partner makes most of the important decisions in your life and you don't have a say about what you need from your life, this will play out in your sex life. If you keep quiet about your needs, you might not get what you need in your sex life. You might find yourself using sex as a tool by withholding it from your relationship. So often, when I ask couples about their sex lives, it seems that one partner is relatively content and the other is silently dissatisfied.

Some couples' sex life reflects a power struggle between two people's needs. If sex sometimes feels like a battle about who did what and when, you need to clear the air by speaking about it openly. A power struggle is only one until it is talked about.

When and how did we become so sexually or intimately disconnected?

The loss of sexual connection can be caused by:
- exhaustion;
- being overworked;
- anxiety and depression;
- feeling too domesticated;
- parenthood; and …
- trauma.

Your state of being creates the context for sex. Feeling exhausted, rushed, chaotic and pressurised is no place for intimacy and sex. Focus on relaxing and resting first. While sex and intimacy can be energising, you need energy to feel sexy and intimate. Sex and intimacy require energy and give energy. Relaxation and enjoyment of life is an essential ingredient for a happy sex life.

Questions to ask about your relationship
- What are some of the biggest negative influences on our sex life?
- How can we invite more relaxed times into our life?
- How can we put energy back into our relationship?

How have my sexual and intimate needs changed over time?

As you change, you need to update each other by speaking openly and honestly about what you desire, prefer, need and want sexually and intimately during the current phase of your life. Honesty about your sexual and intimate needs is a gift to your relationship and your constant contribution to remaining sexually and intimately bonded. Abuse or judgment in this space in moments of hurt and anger are a violation of your relationship's safety. As you grow in life, you should constantly share your needs, desires and preferences to be seen sexually throughout the life of your relationship.

The following questions can guide you during this sensitive conversation:
- Can you describe a pattern of sexual activity that has changed for you? How and why have your sexual preferences changed?
- What you would like to have more of sexually or intimately at this point in your life?
- What turns you on at this point in your life?
- What more would you like sexually?

WHAT TO DO

To increase your sexual and intimate satisfaction, try any of the following new behaviours:

Stop making excuses

The most common excuses couples use to not have sex are:
- We are too tired to have sex.
- We never have time for sex – we are too busy.
- We have children and don't have time for sex.
- We are too old for sex.
- We are too stressed and work too hard to have sex.
- We are never alone.
- We have been together for too many years.
- Sex is no longer important to us.
- I feel too unattractive for sex.

Whereas all of your excuses are part of your reality, it is simply too comfortable to hide behind them instead of making the changes you need to make. Let the opposite of every excuse be a starting point for change. Obvious solutions to the excuses listed above, then, would be:
- We need to rest and relax more to have more sex.
- We need to make time in our busy schedules to have sex.
- We need to spend time away from our children to have more sex.
- We are never too old for sex.
- We need to focus on recharging so that we can have sex.

SEX AND INTIMACY

- We need to make time to be alone.
- We need to make sex a priority again.
- We need to reconnect sexually again, with ourselves and with each other.
- I need to make myself more attractive to feel sexy again.

No therapist can give you time or energy or space. You need to define and take the actions you need to create a space for sex and intimacy. If you have children, think of times in which you can be alone and book time for your relationship like you book time for your children's activities. If you are always tired and stressed, focus on putting energy back into your relationship. If you always go to bed at different times, you need to change your routines and patterns for more shared time in your bedroom. Do you know how to do this?

Questions to ask about your relationship
- Which common excuses do we make for not having sex or being intimate?
- Which steps can we take to move in the direction of sex and intimacy?
- When and how can we make time for sex and intimacy in our busy lives?

Stop being sexually lazy

It seems that most couples have a graph in their minds that looks like this:

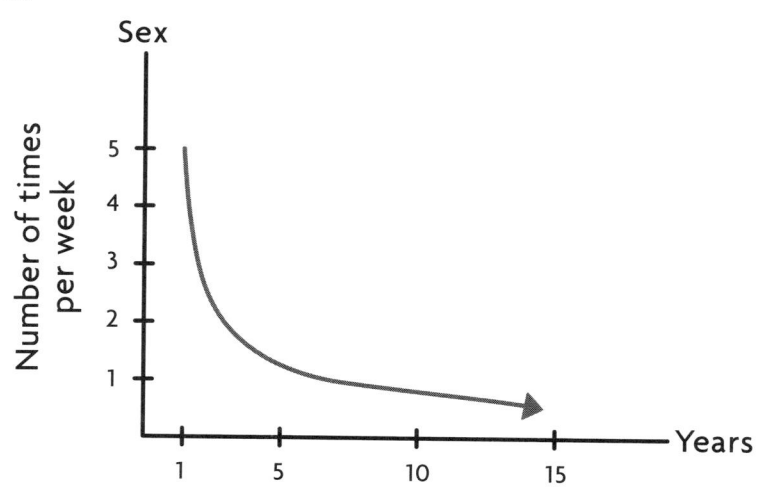

This sad graph is a hiding place for many couples. At social events, I often hear couples joke about the decline in their sex life to make it more acceptable. We look for consensual validation that it is okay, when it is not. We give ourselves permission to become lazy and not have sex for months on end, and we think this is okay. The problem is that even though we joke about it, deep down it doesn't feel okay.

The truth is that not having sex for a week or two feels like an alarm bell in most people's minds. The feeling of disconnection and worry we feel when less and less sex becomes okay always sends an alarm bell to our minds. It triggers thoughts such as, 'Why are we not having sex?', 'Who is going to make the next move?', 'Does he no longer find me attractive?', and 'Is there something wrong with our relationship?' And, the biggest question: 'Is there something wrong with me?'

If you have become sexually lazy, it means you are neglecting your relationship. If your questions about where you partner is have no answers, you need to get sexually active. Extended periods in a sexually disconnected relationship affect our sense of self and the well-being of our relationships.

Questions to ask about your relationship
- Have we become sexually lazy? Why?
- What can we do to become sexually active and vibrant again?

Change your physical space

The feeling of the physical space in which you are intimate and have sex can enhance or hinder your sexual and intimate experience. Sex needs a context that speaks of invitation, safety, warmth, fun and excitement. The context must speak to you of sex and intimacy. That context is different for everyone. A space full of children and animals, or that speaks of chaos, does not make you feel like sex. Electronic devices and televisions should be banned from bedrooms. Consider changing your physical space to invite intimacy and sex.

Questions to consider
- Does our bedroom speak of sex and intimacy?
- In which spaces do we enjoy having sex?
- Which changes we can make to our physical space to receive more sexual messages?
- Where else would we like to have more sex and intimacy?

Make sex and intimacy your priority

The belief that sexual desire and activity should happen spontaneously is simply not realistic (except if you are permanently on holiday). In a time-pressured, busy life, sex and intimacy need to remain a priority if they are to survive. This means that you need to keep sex in your thoughts and actions and not forget the value of being sexually and intimately connected.

Thinking about sex and making time for intimacy is important for any relationship. Sex and intimacy should move between first and third place on your priority list, along with communication. If you struggle to keep sex a priority, you are either making excuses and have become sexually lazy, or you are neglecting your relationship.

> **AN EXERCISE FOR YOUR RELATIONSHIP**
> - Make a list of the current (general) priorities in your life and compare notes.
> - Make a list of your the priorities for your relationship and compare notes.

Questions to ask about your relationship
- Where does sex rate on our priority list, if it ranks at all?
- How can we keep sex and intimacy high on our list of priorities?

Share your fantasies

Fantasising about sex can help to recharge sexual desire.

Fantasy is one of your main tools for arousal. Fantasies are the imaginings, visions and dreams of the sexual mind. They are harmless imaginings and should not be judged, but rather embraced as a natural and real part of any healthy relationship. They are not about being open-minded or sexually liberal – they are a simple tool for arousal, and not an invitation to abandon your boundaries.

Sharing your sexual fantasies and turning them into reality are two different processes. Consider turning your fantasies as a tool for increased arousal into reality carefully, because making your fantasies a reality may change their form and feel. You risk losing a powerful but harmless tool for arousal, because reality and fantasy are often not the same experience for most. The fantasy holds more power as a tool for arousal than its reality.

Questions to consider
- Which sexual fantasies would we like to share with each other?
- Which of my or your fantasies really turn me on?

Change your sexual focus

As with sharing your sexual needs and wants, speaking openly about your sexual preferences in terms of positions and roles can redirect your relationship. Realising that sex and intimacy swim in a big pool of varied activity might open your mind to many other satisfying sexual processes that you might have been missing out on. Move your primary focus from penetration and ejaculation to increased enjoyment, pleasure and satisfaction. Removing dominant ideas of how sex should play out, and creating your own satisfying encounters, could greatly improve your experience of sex.

Questions to consider
- Which sexual positions would we like to try?
- Into which sexual activities would we like to invite each other?
- Which role-plays interest us?

Kiss, kiss, kiss

If you are struggling to connect physically or sexually, remember that kissing can be an instant pathway to closeness and physical connection. Kissing is your tool for connection during times of sexual disconnection. Shift your focus from arousal, ejaculation and penetration and kiss each other until your feel your bodies moving in the same direction. Kissing is a stepping stone to arousal and sends the message that we want to be with each other, that we are desired and are connecting.

Get naked

Spend time naked in an environment that feels safe and comfortable. Your intention is to enjoy each other's bodies as much as you enjoy the company. Move away from an overemphasis on arousal, which adds pressure to your experience. Rather focus on stimulation, enjoyment and relaxation. Spend time naked and do whatever you feel like with the time you have. This doesn't have to involve arousal, penetration and ejaculation. Your intention is to reconnect physically and emotionally, and awaken your desire for each other. Your main focus is to have a relaxing, fun and enjoyable experience without your clothes on.

Questions to ask about your relationship
- When and how can we make time to get naked?
- When we get naked, what can we do together that will bring us closer?

Stroke and caress each other

AN EXERCISE FOR YOUR RELATIONSHIP

- Get naked and take turns to stroke and caress each other's bodies (for about 10 to 30 minutes per person). It is often best to move from the face and neck downwards. Your focus can be non-genital and genital.
- Your aim is to create an awareness of which type of strokes and caresses are most arousing. Pleasure (not sexual performance) is your focus. Try to establish some emotional intimacy, rather than aim for sexual release. It is important not to rush this process. Slow it down; focus on arousing and pleasuring each other for as long as you need to. Try to stay mindful of your body's responses in the moment. Intercourse is not the aim, but if the arousal progresses to a need for intercourse and you both feel it is consensual, it can be good. Your focus is on giving each other pleasure.
- Do not hesitate to stop the process when you feel you need to, or have had enough. A simple 'okay', 'no', or 'I enjoyed this ...' can signal that moment.

Connect your mind and body

To remain in the moment during sex and intimacy, you need to keep your mind and body connected. If you connect with my mind, my body will follow; if you connect with my body, it connects our minds.

As one of the main pathways to connection, sex requires your mind and body to be connected. It requires presence. Switching your mind off when you are touched sexually can be harmful to you, and is often an action and experience associated with abuse.

It is difficult to show real physical interest and arousal when you mind is not engaged. If you live in a space where you mind and body do not connect, sex will be driven by either your mind or your body. Maintaining that disconnection between your mind and body can become problematic over time.

You need to connect not only to yourself, but also to your partner's mind, body and soul. To connect to your body, you need to get to know your body. To get to know your mind, you need to work on exploring and acknowledging your thoughts.

Questions to consider
- How can I stay present in my mind and body during sex or intimacy?
- How can we assist each other to stay present during sex?

Make yourself more attractive

Sex is often about attraction. To increase or maintain your desirability for each other, it is important to remain physically and emotionally attractive to each other and to yourself. To up your attraction, take any of the following steps:

Become more attractive to yourself
Feeling unattractive to yourself creates a disconnection in your intimate and sex life. You wonder why anyone would want to touch you, make love to you or be with you if you do not feel good enough for yourself.

A loss of attraction starts often starts with you and not with your relationship. You know which changes you need to make to ensure you become more attractive to yourself. If you need to start exercising or eat better, take action. Your intention is to define and step into your own desirability. Often, it is not your weight or appearance, but rather the experience of your body, that can rekindle the attraction.

Keep yourself physically attractive for each other
It is sensitive to speak the truth about your loss of attraction to your partner, but it is also your invitation to make a change. Keeping quiet about a loss of attraction creates other problems in your relationship, such as distance and disconnection. You have a responsibility to your intimate and sex life to speak gently about a loss of physical attraction and to support each other in making the changes you need to get your groove back.

Spend some time apart
Attraction grows during periods of separation. Often, I hear about couples who have more sex and become more intimate after being apart. If you have ever wondered why you feel a need for sexual or intimate closeness after a business trip or time apart, it is because of

the power of distance. Separation and time apart ignite your sexual desire. Time apart creates a longing for each other that drives your need to get closer to each other.

Do not share your bodily functions
Bodily functions and private grooming processes are a source of unattractiveness for many couples. Be mindful of how a lack of privacy during your own personal processes can erode your desire for each other.

Become emotionally attractive
At the heart of a loss of attraction is the loss of emotional attraction. A loss of attraction is often more about losing emotional attraction than physical attraction. When you lose your temper or treat people disrespectfully, you become unattractive over time. Ego, selfish behaviour, unawareness and insensitivity are unattractive to most people.

It is simple: loss of attraction = loss of respect. If you lose respect, you often lose attraction, which will directly impact on your sex and intimate life. No matter how good your look, if you don't respect your partner you don't feel that burning desire to be close.

Show some manners
How you treat others and how you behave in their company can cause a loss of attraction. Showing some manners is not only about having good table manners and eating with your mouth closed, but about treating all beings as you would like to be treated – with respect, interest, kindness and consideration.

Questions to ask about your relationship
- What can we do to become more attractive to each other?
- How can we support each other on our own journeys of becoming more attractive to each other?

Know your erogenous zones

AN EXERCISE FOR YOUR RELATIONSHIP

Well known as an exercise used by sex therapists all over the world, marking your erogenous zones on a body chart like the ones on page 127 can indicate whether you understand each other's bodies. Erogenous zones are the areas of your body that enjoy stimulation and cause an increase in arousal. Your erogenous zones can change over time, so checking in with each other through dialogue or charting is important for continued sexual connection. For sexual experiences to be satisfying, it is essential to know your body's erogenous zones and those of your partner. Without showing each other your body charts, mark your own, and then your partner's, sensitive spots. Compare notes.

Increase your intimacy

If you need greater intimacy in your relationship, consider any of the following actions:
- kissing;
- touching;
- bathing or showering together;
- holding hands;
- looking into each other's eyes; or
- Sharing your intimate emotions and thoughts.

Intimacy does not happen in a rushed, stressed space. Stress and exhaustion are the enemies of intimacy. Relax before you try to become more intimately focused. A space that speaks of slowing down and not rushing off anywhere, in which you don't function according to a time frame, is what you need to create. From a relaxed space and an uninterrupted and private time, you will start to feel the energy of intimacy.

Questions to ask about your relationship
- How can we create relaxed spaces for our relationship that are not ruled by time?
- Which intimate gestures or behaviours make us feel more intimately connected?

SEX AND INTIMACY

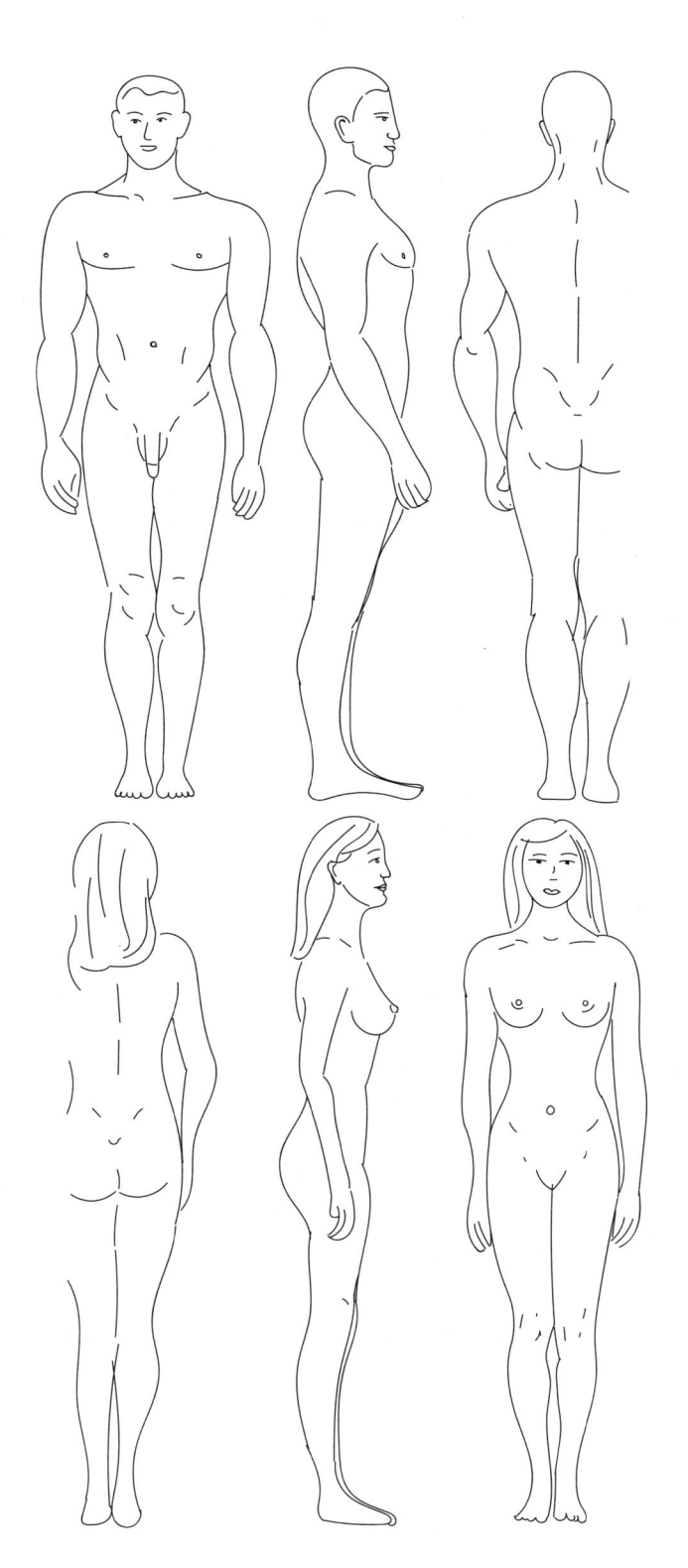

Go on regular dates

A date is your opportunity to be alone and to connect. A date gives your relationship priority over all of the other people and activities in your life and reminds your of the importance of connection and sex. It is a time booked for connection and enjoyment, a time for checking in with each other and your relationship. Often, if you go on a date feeling disconnected, it seems better to focus on having fun and enjoying yourself. In the process of enjoyment, you might find yourselves moving closer.

Going on regular, enjoyable dates has never done any couple any harm. If you are always busy, you need to book some dates in advance. A date should be fun and light and serious all at the same time, because as you start sharing your truth during your date and start seeing each other, you will feel closer. A date that reconnects you is the best place in the world!

Questions to ask about your relationship
- How can we make regular dates a part of our life?
- When is a good time for us to go on a date?
- Which kind of dates would interest us and enrich our relationship?

Increase your romance

Being a romantic myself, I strongly support the processes of romance ... the forgotten expressions of love. If you have worked successfully towards a better intimate and sex life and you want to raise your standards, try to put some romance into your relationship. Romance is a conscious act or expression of your love, respect and support for each other. It is a creative and considered expression of your love. Sadly, most couples extend romantic gestures only when they are in trouble.

The perception that romance happens spontaneously, as it does in the movies, is simply not true for most couples. Romance needs consideration and planning. You need to think carefully about what your partner might appreciate and love, and plan your romantic gesture with your partner in mind. Your intention is to acknowledge

your partner and send this message: 'I see you, love you and appreciate you.' To do this, you need to think about which restaurant he would love, or cook her favourite meal. If you want to impress your partner with some romantic gestures, here are some of the more obvious ideas:
- extended periods of French kissing;
- candlelit dinners;
- picnics;
- holding hands;
- flowers; or
- leaving cards, notes and letters.

As meaningful as these actions can be, the real romantic gestures are more emotional than material. A letter in which you have taken the time to think about your relationship and your partner, for example, is worth a lot. Acts that speak of seeing and knowing each other, and of consideration, become memories we value.

Questions to consider in choosing romantic gestures include
▸ Which gestures would speak of romance for me?
▸ Which romantic gifts would my partner enjoy?

Work around the not-so-sexy roles

Partners take on many different roles in the same relationship. We are lovers, friends, parents and administrators.

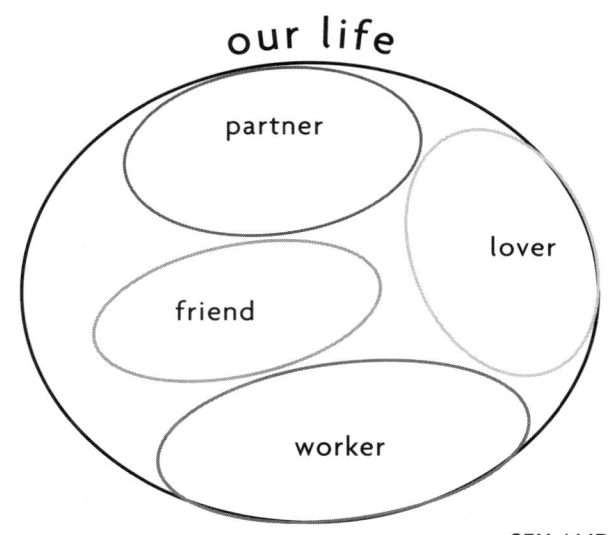

our life
- partner
- lover
- friend
- worker

When we become parents, we feel our roles change. We find ourselves parenting a child while missing the friendship and partnership of our relationship. When you take on a building project, you become project managers and administrators. The more you take on in your life, the more domesticated you find yourself becoming. Unfortunately, the roles of partner and lover often fade away.

'We are great friends, but don't have sex anymore.'

'We work well as a team, but we no longer connect.'

'We are great parents to our children, but never have time for our relationship.'

'We co-habit very well, but I feel lonely in our relationship.'

If you become great administrators, parents or friends but you no longer have sex and intimacy, you have lost each other along the way. Whereas life requires administration and parenting and friendship, no relationship can survive without the connection of intimacy and sex.

In time, most couples become better parents than partners. Having children adds to your life's administrative load; we find ourselves becoming great team players, without sex or intimacy.

Most couples complain about:
- too much domestication, organisation and planning;
- too many routines;
- too much stress (work, finances);
- parenthood, first and foremost;
- having too little time for their relationship; and …
- having no time for themselves.

Your solution is to put your relationship back into the space of your life. If you do not prioritise your relationship, it will always come last. Nobody can do this for you; it is a conscious process of making space and time for your roles as lovers, friends and partners. A relationship in which you never have time alone or space without interruptions will ultimately run into trouble. Give your relationship some space in your full and busy lives, and don't let sex and intimacy fall off the page of your life.

Questions to ask about your relationship
- Which roles dominate our intimate and sex lives?
- When and how can we make more space for our relationship?

IN CLOSING

Sex is one of the most important pathways to connection.

Not having sex with a partner robs your relationship of opportunities for closeness and enjoyment. Sex and intimacy are reminders of your love and desire for each other. It reminds you about the importance of being connected and seen.

Your sexual satisfaction and connection should grow as you grow over time. This is less about frequency; it is the experience of your intimate and sexual life that really matters.

Chapter 6

dating (and meeting new people)*

Just because two people have a connection and get along, does not mean that they should date each other. Really knowing each other goes far beyond a connection.

In the process of meeting people, you have to relate the stories about who you think you are and what you do for a living. But it seems that when we move beyond our lives' usual stories, we find our truest connections.

THE FIRST ROUND

When you meet someone, you look for moments of attraction, similarities and connections. We connect on many levels: physical, intellectual, sexual, cultural, spiritual and emotional. Most of us search for the following:
- physical attraction
- an intelligent mind
- independence, a career, security
- a cultural and social fit
- an emotional connection; and
- a spiritual match.

---

* Although this chapter was written for people interested in, or in the process of, dating, its lessons are relevant for all situations that involve meeting new people.

Often, we move from physical attraction to an intellectual connection to dating, but this is simply not enough of a basis for building a new relationship. Do not be blinded by a physical and intellectual connection. Look beyond the initial attraction and get to know the person you want to be with – with great awareness.

AWARENESS IS YOUR PROTECTION

What you cannot see can surprise and hurt you. Being aware is all about seeing yourself and the people you meet with greater clarity and perception. The more accurately you see people, the better the decisions you can make about what you allow into your life.

To increase your awareness during the process of meeting people and finding the true and lasting love of your life, start with any of the following:

For starters, use that checklist

Often we use a checklist of characteristics, preferences and deal-breakers for dating. This checklist follows on from the first round of obvious attraction, and contains detailed and superficial preferences. It seems everyone has that checklist: he must not be a smoker, she must not be religious, he must have big hands, she must be family oriented …

When people speak about what connects them to, and puts them off, people, I am constantly amazed by the extent to which aware and intelligent people can be put off by what might seem like small things. He had ugly feet; she smokes; his feet were small – these seem to be real reasons for some to withdraw their interest. Small things can have big effects. I smile when I hear, 'I don't want to be judgemental, but …' A small thing for one person is a big thing for another. So, what may seem like small and superficial things appear to constitute the nature of attraction. It seems very important to know what you like and dislike in life – particularly when you want to meet new people and build a future together.

Your checklist is most likely judgmental (and the last thing the world needs is more judgment); often, the first round of attraction and interest can be very superficial. It is important to know what you like and to take a position, as small things can become big things over time. A person without opinions can be dangerous. So, know what you prefer before you enter the dating game.

Have expectations, needs, wants and preferences. Expectations can hurt you, but take a position. It is dangerous not to. Know where you will draw the line.

Understand the layers of attraction

It took me years to understand the layers of attraction. When I speak to people about their dating experiences, I often ask what they find attractive in a person and what would make them go on a second, or subsequent, date.

Aware, intelligent adults are usually impressed by what they see. They want more if the person is physically attractive and comes across as intelligent. But attraction has many layers. It is important to see how attraction works in you, and why. In other words, it is important not to be blinded by what you find attractive in another and forget to look at what is happening to you during the dating process. It is important not to be blinded by your wants and your need to be in a relationship – and not to switch off the cues from your mind, heart or soul.

This awareness is important as the first few rounds of meeting someone can be deceptive. It is in the beginning that you need to keep an open mind and maintain your awareness. The fact that meeting someone has moved and excited you, does not mean that he or she needs to be in your life in the long term. Take your time and look at what really connects you. Are seeing this person accurately, or do you just need or want him or her desperately?

The experience of physical attraction and intellectual connection on a first or second date cannot, and does not, need to be measured – it will reside in you as an overwhelming sense of knowing. It feels like a definite yes in your mind and heart – no analysis needed. It may be a good start, but look beyond it to see the layers of attraction.

For most people, the layers of attraction work like this:

Firstly, and most obviously, the person needs to be more or less attractive physically for you to continue the pursuit (this attraction often happens instantly).

Secondly, to find another's mind attractive, you need to find common interests and be able to speak to each other with ease. For most, how the conversation goes is a sign of intelligence.

Next, the thing that people will only admit to their closest friends and therapists, maybe, is that after they have established the initial attraction, their detailed, secret checklist kicks in. What the person does for a living, where he or she lives and, sometimes, what he or she drives can also matter. If these things matter to you, just be honest. Make your superficial list from the start and put it behind you to get to the more important layers. We all know that the world needs less superficiality and judgment, and more authentic truth. Even if your preferences may seem judgmental to others, know what you like, prefer, want and desire from the start. Maybe this *is* being truthful.

Physical and intellectual connections are not enough to build a relationship. Is it really enough for you that the person you are interested in is attractive and intelligent, and has some kind of career? It seems that we date people on their potential and overlook their reality – their most important part.

At the heart of your future

At the heart of your dating awareness should be a focus on emotional attractiveness. Whereas emotions, for some, are all about the soft stuff and are seen, possibly, as overrated, the truth is that the emotional ways of the person you are interested in will have the biggest impact on your experience of being in that relationship. This is all about good energy and can save you from constant surprises, disappointments and heartache.

- You need to switch on to emotional attractiveness, which is about:
- how the person engages with all human beings;
- how kind, gentle and generous she or he can be;
- how he or she manages his or her close relationships;

- how the person engages with his or her emotions;
- how honest and straightforward (but kind) the person is;
- how often the person loses his or her temper;
- whether he or she has an understanding of what really matters in life;
- whether he or she is not overly materialistic, but generous in spirit;
- how self-reliant and responsible the person is for his or her life choices; and
- whether the person is interested in growth, awareness and movement in life.

Emotional attraction is the centre of lasting attraction. How a person engages with his or her emotions will be at the heart of the future experience of your relationship. When you are emotionally attractive, it radiates through all of your layers and shines through your eyes. Losing your temper irresponsibly and taking things out on others, blaming others for what you feel, or showing interest and then becoming unavailable emotionally is simply not emotionally attractive. This kind of emotional irresponsibility will destroy every attractive aspect of your relationship.

In simple terms, if you find a person hot and intelligent, take your time to find out what he or she is really like emotionally. Your happiness, and that of your relationship, will be determined by the emotional experience of being in your relationship. To put it even more simply, if the person you are dating is hot, but speaks to you or others with disrespect, he or she will quickly become less hot.

PREPARING YOURSELF FOR DATING

If you are ready to start dating with a greater awareness of what attracts you and what a true connection looks like for you, you need to ask yourself some questions in preparation:

What is dating really about for you?

Most of us have dating stories, and can speak for hours about our dating experiences – the good, the bad and the scary. Dating can be as educational as it is entertaining.

When you date, you expose your innermost parts to someone new to be accepted and liked, so dating can be a huge learning experience about yourself. The desire to be liked can fill us with all kind of anxieties, so dating can show you how rejection and acceptance live in you. It reveals your emotional ways and vulnerabilities. In the process of seeking acceptance and encountering possible rejection, parts of you will come to fore with which you hadn't connected before.

Whereas dating can be a daunting exercise for most people, and feels hugely personal, it often says more, ironically, about the society in which you live than about yourself. When you embark on the journey of dating and meeting new people, you will most likely expose yourself to what is in the societies around you. Dating does not have to be personal, because it is also cultural. You will catch a glimpse of the culture that surrounds you – the beautiful, the bad and, sometimes, the scary.

Dating is about filtering through the dominant cultures of your society to get what you want. If you are not ready for what is around you, you may not be ready for dating.

Dating as social research

Dating should no longer be called dating, but social research. In social research, the researcher observes life as an outsider. It is not about absorbing a life that is not yours – it is about standing on the sidelines and observing what goes by before getting involved. This is what the process of dating can be like.

A very good friend once taught me about observation versus absorption, a lesson that, truly, saved me future pain during my own shocking dating career. She often spoke about her mother in ways that suggested that her mother was less on the motherly than the toxic side of life. She told me how she would prepare herself to spend time with her mother by imagining that a golden bubble surrounded her when she was in her mother's company. This taught me not only about toxic human behaviour, but also about how to protect myself against what I do not want in relationships. I learnt how to observe, and not absorb, other people's behaviour.

An observant mindset can be a useful dating tool. Observation is about looking closely at what is in your society, what every interaction is doing to you, what you find attractive and why. Absorption is about taking on other people's emotions and behaviour, in which you have no say and over which you have no control. Absorption can be dangerous. Rather learn to observe as much as you can.

How the person you are dating behaves towards you says more about them than you; you cannot control another person's choices. So, instead of taking dating personally, see it as your opportunity to learn about human behaviour.

Defining dating as the chance to meet new and, sometimes, interesting, people may change how you experience it and allow you to observe, and not absorb, everything that comes your way. It may be easier to go on a date with an interest in others instead of an overwhelming fear of rejection. If dating is about meeting new people and getting a glimpse of society, why do we take it so personally?

If you take your dating experiences personally, you need to ask yourself some questions:

Are you ready for dating?

I am often reminded that most happy, single people suddenly go into therapy when they enter a new relationship: 'I was perfectly fine until I started dating …'

The reasons for the sudden visit to your therapist could be two-fold. Firstly, you may be dating someone who treats you badly or makes you doubt yourself. For some reason, we allow behaviour in intimate relationships that we would never allow in any of our other relationships. In our desperate need to love and be loved, we turn a blind eye to the warning signs. Observe whether the person you are dating is making you doubt or question yourself. Ask yourself, 'Is the doubt I feel a reflection of something I need to work on, or is it a reflection of what the person I am dating is doing to me?'

Secondly, there is nothing like dating to trigger our emotional sensitivities. Dating seems to push all of our buttons involving rejection, abandonment, not being chosen, and being pushed aside. It holds the power of rejection, even if it is not really about rejection. If you have a sensitivity to rejection, it might be better to date yourself first by exploring and overcoming your emotional triggers, otherwise dating may feel like a relentless and scary rejection experience.

Do you like yourself enough to be liked and loved?

You need to work on liking and loving yourself before you can consider the affection and love of another. If you are not sure whether you like or love yourself, you will accept exactly that in return: someone who treats you as badly as you treat yourself. If you neglect yourself, do not be surprised if you new partner starts neglecting you. Dating starts from a place of self-love. If you think that someone else's love will fix your dislike of yourself, you will accept less than you deserve from the start. And this has never made anyone feel better about themselves. Ask yourself, 'Do I have enough self-love and respect to accept love from another?'

Are your boundaries strong enough?

If you don't like or love yourself, you may have weak boundaries. Do you know what is acceptable to you and where you draw the line with behaviour you don't want? If you experience something you don't like, do you know how to communicate this?

Are you ready to step outside your comfort zone?

If you are single, and stuck in a pattern of going to work, watching series on your couch and hanging with your 'couple' friends, it is time to step out of your comfort zone.

Stepping out of your comfort zone means breaking your usual patterns of movement. It is time to accept and create invitations, and step into new zones, because dating does not happen in a comfort zone. If your friends never introduce you to new and interesting people, you need to create your own invitations. This means thickening the plot of your social life and either inviting people into your life or getting invited into others' lives. Think creatively about how you can increase the energy of your life.

You have to step out of your comfort zone to meet someone new.

How can I meet new and interesting people? What kind of social experiments would I like to create for others? How can I invite people into my life? Am I ready to step out of my comfort zone to meet someone new? Am I ready to give up my comforts and feel the discomfort of dating?

Can you spend time on your own?

If the idea of being on your own makes you anxious, you are not ready for dating. If you cannot be on your own, or you avoid being on your own, rather date yourself before you go on any dates. If you fill your life with constant activity and people because you fear being on your own, it means you believe that your life will only get better with a partner. You cannot imagine being happy without being in a relationship, and your desperate need for a relationship will make you accept less than you deserve. Your need to be in a relationship will always override your need to take care of yourself – if you meet someone who is not suited to you or treats you badly, you may choose to turn a blind eye just to stay in the relationship. Your need will outweigh your logic.

You need to learn to get comfortable with your own company before you can accept the company of others. Learn what it means to love and have a relationship with yourself before you start dating.

Which dating method do you prefer?

You need to decide which method of dating you prefer. Would you prefer to expand your social life and start inviting people into your life, or do you feel brave enough to put yourself on the Internet and join an online dating site? Either way, you need to accept that you need to be exposed to what is out there to meet your match.

Old-school dating

Internet dating seldom starts with going on good old dates. If you do not like the process of Internet dating and would prefer to meet people in person, you need to focus on expanding your life. In simple terms, this means inviting new people into your life and creating more activity in your life. Old-school dating is about meeting new and interesting people who may become your friends or, hopefully, your match. Sitting on your couch with the remote control is not going to yield a new partner.

The expectation of your friends and family helping you to meet someone may be wishful thinking. This expectation may only become true if you have asked, clearly, for their assistance. If you do not announce to your circles that they need to help you to find your partner, only you can make it happen. If you need it, you need to create it. So, instead of waiting to be invited, make some noise – start inviting the people you know into your life and ask them to bring people with them whom you do not know. Think of experiences, activities and events you would like to share with others, and invite people to come with you. Do not be discouraged if people don't rise to the occasion. Keep moving and shaping new experiences that will excite you no matter what. In all that activity and newness, you may just meet someone really interesting.

The truth is that people often meet new partners when they move outside the circles of their everyday life. The focus on dating seems completely misguided – the focus on having a rich and interesting life seems so much more important and relaxing! Taking on a new interest that excites and delights you will surround you with like-minded people. It's a promising start.

Internet dating

Many people – women and men – cannot imagine going out to a club or bar to meet people. Even if they live in a big city, they express no interest in going out to do so. For many others, there is no club or bar to go to. How then, can you meet a partner? Internet dating seems to be the logical solution.

You can date on the Internet from the comfort of your home or phone with the safety of a protective boundary. You can make decisions about who you like and dislike and who you want to talk to. All you need is a keyboard or pad. It is dating with a lot of control: you can simply block, delete or switch off if it isn't working for you.

For most, the process of Internet dating does not feel like dating. Because it exposes you to a higher number of people in a much shorter time, it is the ultimate form of 'social research'. You do a great deal of filtering and chatting before you even consider a date.

It's like fishing in a big pond – a few fish may bite, but you may never catch the big one. It reminds me of fishing with my father when I was a small boy. A lot of preparation, the wait for a bite, and sometimes – if you are lucky – some interesting stories or a fish to make you proud. Sometimes, the fish you almost had disappeared into the deep blue sea.

Internet dating takes up a lot of time and energy, sometimes with no positive results. Because it takes so much time and energy, it has an expiry date. So, it is wise to take breaks from it as you can reach a point of too much exposure and expended energy.

Internet dating should not hold the power of rejection, because the biggest part of Internet dating is filtering, and more filtering, through what is in your environment. Filtering means you sifting through the 'bites' you receive, making carefully considered choices. The filtering process takes the form of photographs and online chatting. It can get pretty time consuming: a lot of chatting with strangers, some moments of truth that, maybe, feel like connection, then more chatting. An Internet dating connection may be just that – a connection on the Internet that does not necessarily translate into a real-life connection.

Internet dating is all about creating choices of, and opportunities for, dates. The more choices you have, the better online dating can feel.

Many people misrepresent themselves, so Internet dating should not make you feel rejected easily: how can you feel rejected by someone who may not even be real?

For some, Internet dating is too superficial; and many prefer feeling someone's energy in person, and find the filtering process wasteful. Others love the social research, the filtering, the crazy chats and the power of instant choice.

The Internet dating filter is big and wide, and looks like this:

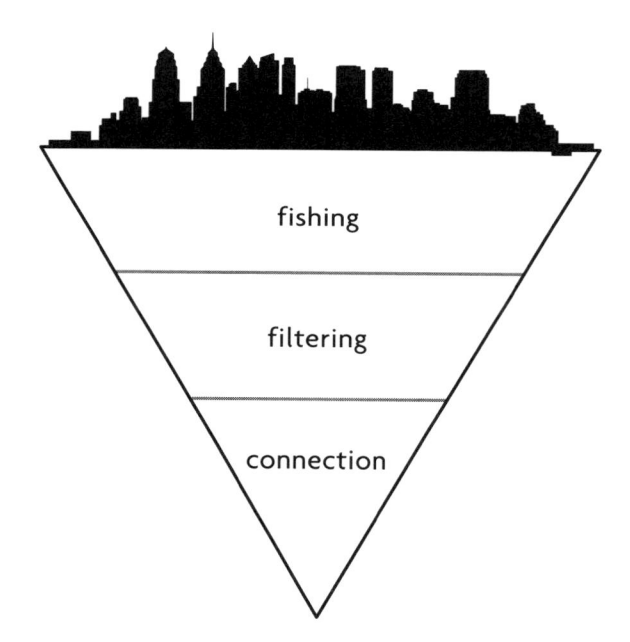

fishing

filtering

connection

How would you like to present yourself?

Deciding how you want to present yourself is at the core of your online dating experience. What is true about you? What matters to you most at this point in your life? Whatever feels true and important to you, at this point in your life, is what you present to others. It is not that difficult to be liked, but it is more important to be honest. Try to present yourself as accurately and honestly as you can, because this is what you expect in return. We are all looking for real, honest connection. If this is what you want too, you need to present yourself with honesty. Honesty is attractive.

If you are honest with yourself, and you don't like what your body looks like at the moment, it would make no sense to post a photograph of you looking hot on that beach in Thailand five years ago. What you project to others will come back to you. If you lie about your realities, you could meet others who lie about theirs. How you present yourself is most likely what you will get in return.

If your ego is too big or too small, you may find yourself attracted to people who love themselves too much. If you like to play the field, you may find yourself in the company of players. If you give the impression that you have wealth or success when you don't, you might arouse the interest of the ones who need saving. If you are dishonest about who you are, do not be surprised if you get lied to. The energy you give is the energy you get.

If you want a relationship with an honest, real and generous person, get real yourself first, and avoid people who take more than they give.

LESSONS LEARNT

With your checklist at the back of your mind, loaded with self-love and some serious self-awareness, and with a plan of action, you could be ready to go on a few dates. In case you think you are, learn some life lessons from people who have been through the dating process.

The following truths may guide you along the way:

A 'maybe' is a 'no'

As superficial as you think your checklist may be, it is mostly about your five senses. Your senses never lie, and cannot be denied. What you see, hear, feel, smell and touch either works for you or doesn't. If you senses say 'no' or 'maybe', it is not going to work for you. Even if your mind lies to you enough to convince you that you could, a 'maybe' cannot live with that smell or look or touch. The truth is that a 'maybe' is always a 'no'. Keep looking for a definite two-way 'yes' from all of your senses.

Age is relevant

When you date someone in his or her twenties and you are in your forties, age is relevant. An age gap of more than 15 years can work in the moment, but in time, the gap seems to grow. You might connect at 45 with a 28 year old, but when one partner turns 38 and another is turning 55, pushing 60, age suddenly feels more relevant. It is not about being ageist. It is about being aware of the reality that two people in two different phases of their lives would want, need and desire different things. If you get involved with someone significantly older or younger than you, you need to manage the reality of age over time.

Distance as a deal-breaker

Meeting and connecting with someone who lives in a different city or country is an important future consideration. Distance has its own energy, and is like a third force in any relationship – it *will* create obstacles. As two people who are really interested in each other and who have a strong connection, you will have to accept that distance creates distance. It is also relevant to acknowledge that the more settled you are in your lives, the more difficult it may become to bring your lives together in the same place when the time comes. No matter how strong your connection, distance will affect it – sometimes to the point of financial and emotional exhaustion.

Substances create false connections, sometimes

You may have met some of your best friends or partners during a wild night of intoxication. On the night, you feel that you have made a real friend or real connection. But meeting the same person again, sober, may change your perception of the connection. Real connections are sober connections. Real connections take time; a real friend or partner will be around in good times and in very sobering ones.

Income is relevant

Being on different socio-economic levels and having different income streams do have an impact on most relationships. Being able to afford to eat at a certain restaurant, or to go on an overseas holiday, is one of many examples that can affect the experience of your relationship if your partner cannot match your expenditure. Like any obstacle, it is not impossible to overcome, but it needs some serious consideration before you get deeply involved. What might be fine in the beginning, could become a source of resentment in the future. Even if one of you gives without expecting something in return, most people like to receive as they give, one day.

You need, or are, what you are attracted to

It is important to recognise that what you find attractive in others, you also carry in, or need, yourself. What you seek in others, you may value most in yourself. And, sometimes, what we seek in others, we lack in ourselves. The person you pursue holds the qualities you think you need to have a better life or be a better person. But being saved, or in need, are not suitable building blocks for starting a relationship.

During this process of dating, I often find that we project what we like about ourselves onto another person. This means that everything that you like or dislike about a person could mirror a past or present part of you. If you dislike some qualities in a person you meet, you may need to look for those same qualities in yourself.

Your generosity is never a problem

The qualities that you are proud of are the qualities with which you should surround yourself. If you are proud of your generous spirit and your giving ways, then surround yourself with people who are also generous and like to reciprocate. These are your kind of people.

Generosity is only a problem in the company of takers. Givers in the company of givers create a life of abundance. But if you give to the point of exhaustion, and often feel upset, angry or resentful that you are not getting what you need from your relationships, you are surrounding yourself with people who are most likely not your kind of people.

When we start to like someone, we often want to give more of ourselves, and our lives, to be liked. Be aware of how and what you give in the first year of a relationship. In this time, you set the tone and feed an expectation that could leave you resentful and exhausted. Reciprocation is a two-way street, and is at the core of a good dating experience and future relationship.

Your emotions never lie

Your mind may get stuck on your dating checklist, but your heart will never lie. You can override your mind with your need to be in a relationship. You can force that circle into a square, but you will know if it does not feel right.

To keep yourself safe during the dating period, you need to switch onto your intuition and remain aware of your emotions. Keeping your eyes open and listening to your gut feeling can save you a lot of hurt.

What do you need to stay aware of when you date? Look at how the process of dating makes you feel. Every negative emotion is a warning, or a direction marker. It tells you what is not good for you or what you don't like. If you are communicating with someone new or are simply spending time with someone you are getting to know, and it is confusing you or upsetting you in any way, you need to take note. Ignoring life's cues at the beginning of a potential relationship can cause a lot of drama and pain.

The question to keep in mind is: How does this person make you feel, and why? Taking a closer look at your emotions while getting to know a person you like can give you many answers.

If dating confuses you, upsets you, hurts you and adds drama to your life, you are, most likely, dating the wrong person or not ready for dating yourself.

It seems better to turn away from experiences that confuse and upset you than to try to be stronger or make sense of them. Turn away from what does not make you feel good. I often find that it is not even that important to make sense of why an experience is confusing or upsetting you. Doing so can hold you for longer in a situation that is not good for you now, and will likely not be good for you in the future. Rather focus your energy on letting go and moving away. Not spending time in situations that do not allow you to be yourself, and that do not make you feel good about yourself, is a form of self-care and self-love.

Charm is a skill

Dating is not always about your ability to perceive: it can be about your ability to be deceived. Because it is about showing the best versions of ourselves first, it is often difficult to distinguish between the real and the charming version of a person. What people present in the first few rounds of dating may not be the real and accurate version of who they are. It may be a version that the person knows will impress you. But maintaining that good impression will not last – no one can sustain a good first impression forever. Getting to know someone takes time.

Projecting good first impressions and charm is a skill you can learn, a skill that is all about knowing what looks good, how to make a good impression, how to speak and present yourself, and how to get what you want. For some, charm and good manners are mixed with the language of popular psychology and self-help books. A person may have the language and manners to impress, but beneath all of that skill is a real person. Your intention should be to see as much of this real person as possible in the shortest time. Don't be fooled by layers of charm, manners and compliments, because his or her actions are what really matter.

Some people are very skilled at deceiving you. No matter how intelligent and aware you are, if a person is good at deception you could be blinded by the light of his or her very good first impression. It is less about your ability to see than about his or her ability to deceive. So, look beyond first impressions and promises of what could be, and try to see the person accurately and in totality. As we all know, nobody is perfect. Wait for the imperfections to show before you make major commitments.

The following situations are great opportunities for seeing the true colours of the person you think you know:
- when they lose their temper;
- when they do not get what they want;
- how they speak about ex-partners or lovers;
- how they conduct their relationships with their families and friends;
- when you have different views about something and you disagree;
- when they deliver extreme judgments of, and opinions about, people; or
- how they treat animals.

Don't get me wrong. Nobody is perfect; obviously, you have to accept certain imperfections from the start. But the big question is: Do you want to, or can you, live with this person?

Ask yourself some serious questions:
- Can, and do, I really want to live with this behaviour?
- What is the meaning of this behaviour?
- What are the implications of accepting this behaviour for my and the relationship's future?

The graph of getting to know someone may look like this:

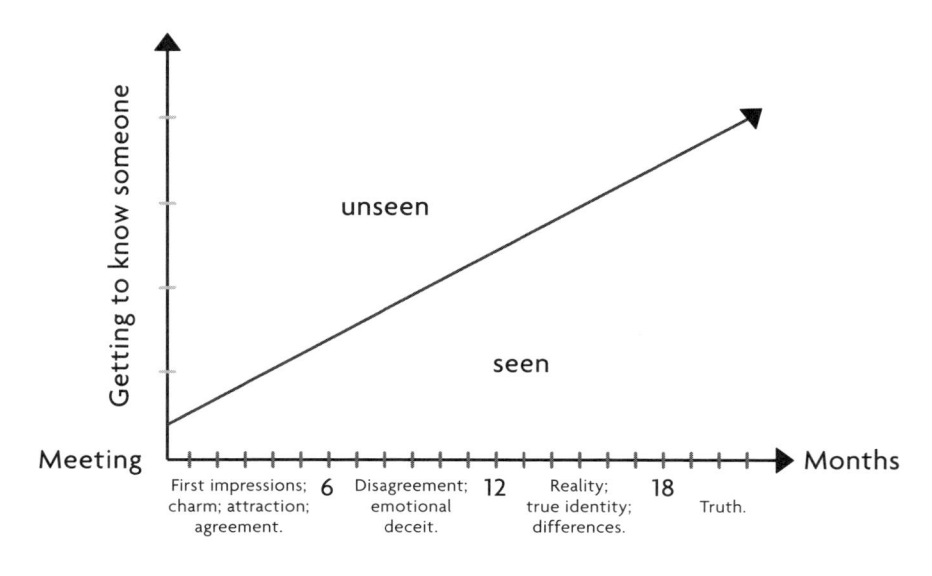

Y-axis: Getting to know someone
X-axis: Meeting → Months

- 6: First impressions; charm; attraction; agreement.
- 12: Disagreement; emotional deceit.
- 18: Reality; true identity; differences.
- Truth.

unseen / seen

In the first six months of a relationship, you get to know each other. You show the best versions of yourselves; there is a lot of agreement. Your first disagreement may happen in the six- to twelve-month period after meeting. Most people only really start seeing each other when they start disagreeing, because disagreement is about not getting what you want and sharing two opinions. As disagreement is part of life and inevitable in any real relationship, it is an important opportunity to get to know each other. When we disagree, we move beyond charm, first impressions and good manners into the space of a real relationship.

Potential is not reality

Don't build a relationship on the potential of a person; rather build it on the reality of what you have. Don't hold on to the potential of the person you like; rather see his or her reality.

You cannot build a relationship on someone's potential. You can only build a relationship on what you have right now. The questions to ask yourself are: What *do* I have right now? What am I really getting from this relationship that I value? What is this relationship doing to me? How does this relationship make me feel?

People with visual minds and imagination – those who can take charge of processes and people, and who are change-makers – often believe in giving a person what they would like to receive in return. But 'I can change this person to give me more of what I want' is a statement of denial; believing it is one of the biggest mistakes you can make while dating or meeting new people. Your focus should always be on what you have, and not on what you might have or think you can create.

No matter what kind of environment or emotions you give someone, if they don't want to change, your giving will make no difference. Doing so may just give the person a reason to take more. The truth is that nobody can change someone if he or she takes no responsibility for his or her own change. **You cannot change another person.** You can only change yourself, and no amount of giving will get you what you want. If you give to receive, you are only sending the message that the less you get, the more you will give. This is dangerously exhausting.

In our human need to be loved, we sometimes get swept up in fantasies and turn a blind eye to the warnings. Sometimes, our desperate need to be loved can blind us to the obvious warnings. Often, we are desperate to stay in, and be defined by, a relationship. This is often why we allow behaviour in an intimate relationship that we would never allow from any of our friends. Why? The people you date, or with who you enter into a relationship, should always have the most important qualities of your best friends.

Moving too fast causes accidents

If you really like someone and feel secure, there's no need to rush. If you feel pressurised by the speed of the interest and emotions, you need to slow down and ask some questions. What's the rush? Why such intense interest so quickly? You may think that rushing is a reflection of your deep and intense connection, but rushing is often a sign of desperation, neediness and mental instability. That overwhelming feeling of being in love could simply be about one person's desperate need to be loved. Someone telling you that he or she loves you or is in love with you in the first month is premature. Real emotions take time to grow.

Being in love is often about need. It should be about truth.

So, when your new interest tells you that he or she is 'in love' with you after very little time, look for the truth of what is going on.

Children as a deal-breaker

Having, or wanting to have, children is an important consideration for any new relationship.

Entering into a relationship that has existing children means becoming a parent or caregiver, even if this was not part of your plan. You will be sharing roles with all the parties involved in the life of a child, and will, most likely, be communicating with ex-partners about child-care arrangements in the future. If you are not ready to be a parent as well as a partner, rather be honest as soon as possible.

If you want to create your own family, and your new partner does not, do not think that you can change his or her mind over time. Accept the truth of the present, and not the potential of the future, and decide whether you can live with it. If you cannot, you need to step away.

Real interest needs no questions

If the person you like is interested in you, you will not feel doubtful or have persistent questions. Real interest requires no analysis or questioning. It sends a clear message in two directions that says 'yes' with certainty. If getting to know someone confuses you and makes you feel uncertain, step away without trying to make sense of it. You cannot make sense of someone else's behaviour or choices without their participation.

A real connection does not require any questioning or analysis. It does not need to be unpacked as it produces an overwhelming feeling – a knowing – that it is true. It is a clear, honest, two-way message, no questions needed. It is the moment of certainty and truth in which two people truly connect. The answer to questions such as, 'Does he really like me?' and, 'Is she truly interested in me?' is 'no'. When you have to ask questions about the person you have met, or feel confused by your interactions with him or her, life is teaching you to stand back and take care. A real connection is a clear message of mutual and consistent interest.

Constant confusion, wondering and waiting are not good for you.
If the interactions with someone you like leave you wondering or make you feel like you are always waiting, then something is wrong with the relationship. Waiting often means that your needs are not being met and that you are waiting for your partner to participate in your needs. A healthy relationship does not make you wait or wonder. You will always feel secure, as you know where you stand.

Inconsistency means constant upsets

Inconsistency causes instability, like a little boat that rocks back and forth on the waves and eventually capsizes.

Inconsistent interest is a bad sign. It is not an act of love and it is not good for you. Real interest is consistently present. Real interest is always hot. Hot and cold behaviour – where alternate interest and lack of interest move in opposite directions – is your cue to step away. Don't waste your time trying to figure out what is going on. Rather focus your energy on detaching and removing yourself from someone who will continue to upset and confuse you.

When it comes to interest, a 'maybe' is always a 'no'.

Bullies, princesses and narcissists are real

The bully, the princess and the narcissist are all one and the same, and they are everywhere. A person with an overinflated sense of self, who believes that his or her right is the only right, will struggle to accept both of your sets of needs in a relationship. On first appearances, they present themselves with charm, good social skills and compliments. But behind that initial show is the person who is always right and always better than others. Often obsessed with their appearance, they see themselves as more special than the rest of the world. They expect to be treated differently, even if they do not treat others with the same respect they expect to receive. Your needs and opinions, especially if they are not in agreement with theirs, are not allowed. Educate yourself about the patterns and ways of the narcissist and stay far away.

Words and actions should always be consistent

We all know the saying that actions speak louder than words. But words and actions should reflect each other. Some people are word magicians, and can use the power of language to impress and entice. But their actions are often where the truth lies. Listen to people's words, but look out for their actions. A gap between words and actions is often a sign of lies and deceit, and is simply an empty promise. Empty promises mean nothing. You cannot build a trusting relationship on them, but you can build a relationship on actions that speak of honesty, respect and responsibility.

Emotional shallowness exists

Some people do not experience emotions in depth. They maintain a very superficial emotional experience and resist looking inwards. They avoid feelings, so they can move in and out of situations easily without feeling or thinking about consequences. When they say they love you, they mean, 'I love you for as long as it feels good and you give me what I want.' For them, love is not a deep, growing or lasting emotion. It is shallow and fleeting and can change at any moment depending on the conditions. It often leaves you with more questions than answers.

Takers are not givers

Some people give to others. Others take more than they give. Being with a generous, considerate spirit is a beautiful thing. If you have a tendency to give, surround yourself with generous people. A person who gives generously, but only on his or her terms and without consideration, is a bully. A charming, egotistical person may wonder what you are going to do for him or her. A taker with ego expects to receive, and has little to give.

Emotional unavailability: don't go there

Some people may be dating, but are not emotionally ready or available for a relationship. If your heart has recently been broken, you live far away, you have recently experienced trauma, or are in the middle of a divorce or separation, then you are neither ready nor emotionally available for dating. Emotional unavailability means that you have recently experienced or are still in the middle of a life transition. In other words, you have recently been through a major change in your life that is still occupying your mind and heart, making you less available for a new relationship. Not having the time or emotional space to engage in your relationship also makes you unavailable. Unavailability is a real and important consideration. Even if you really like someone and have a great connection, if either of you is not available now, you need to step away.

IN CLOSING

If you want an intimate relationship, you have to date. The processes of dating are full of beautiful personal lessons and eye-opening warnings about relationships in general. The dating journey requires preparation and serious consideration. Your best tool is your intuition. Your ability to listen to yourself and act upon what you hear will protect you. So, start by dating yourself. To meet others, you have to meet yourself first, and know what it means to love yourself.

Chapter 7

loving yourself

We have all heard that the most important relationship you will ever have is the relationship with yourself. If you want to have a relationship with yourself, it needs to be a loving relationship. It makes sense that, if you don't know or love yourself, you might have difficulty accepting love or attention from others. What happens in all of your relationships starts with the way in which you love and take care of yourself. It is a simple equation that, if you don't love yourself, you will accept less than you deserve. You will accept what you think you are worth. When you value yourself and think of yourself as worthy, you will accept only what you are worth. It is relationship logic.

Beauty attracts beauty.

Loving ourselves, despite the obvious logic, seems difficult to put into practice, however. It seems that the idea of loving ourselves feels removed from us – like something we have heard of, but never seen. The mystery of self-love remains unsolved as most of us fill our lives with the obvious solutions like exercising or eating well. Despite our best attempts, we still don't feel this mysterious feeling of self-love, no matter how hard we exercise and how well we eat. We run from yoga to work to gym, and end up feeling more exhausted than energised. We are left with more questions than answers, so our pursuit of that undefined loving relationship often loses momentum. We get busy with making changes, but over time nothing feels different, except that we are doing more.

Because of the vagueness of the idea of self-love, it is not surprising that I often get questions such as these in therapy:

- What does it mean to have a relationship with myself?
- How do I have a relationship with myself?
- I do not know how to love myself. What does it really mean to do so?

Despite the number of self-help books that tell us how to love ourselves, doing so seems like a foreign concept to most of us. When people seek to have a better relationship with themselves, the advice they often receive is …

- step into or live your truth.
- love yourself.
- live a life that you can be proud of; and
- take better care of yourself.

But what does this mean? How do you live the idea of loving yourself?

For many years, I have looked closely at the processes that change people's relationships with themselves. Often I wonder: how can someone who really sees themselves, who has such great self-awareness, not make the changes they need to feel better? Why do we spend so much time trying to understand ourselves without feeling any better about who we are? Why is self-awareness not enough?

The truth is that being self-aware is just the introduction to loving yourself. Loving yourself requires action, not hours of self-analysis. It is in our doing and not our speaking that we really change our experience of ourselves and start to feel our own love.

The following five changes seem to hold power for most people:

1. CHANGE THE WAY YOU SPEAK

Changing the way you speak to yourself about yourself is one of the most important steps you can take to feel stronger and better about who you are. The way you speak to yourself internally shapes the experience not only of yourself, but of your entire life. To change your experience of yourself, start by questioning your definitions of who you think you are.

Question your ideas about yourself

You would be surprised by how many intelligent, thinking people do not think they are intelligent enough. They have interesting jobs and can tell some interesting stories, but they are 'not as intelligent as others'. They tell me how 'other people' are more intelligent than they are.

The idea that some people are more intelligent than you is most likely not true. It is one of many ideas you were not born with, but received along the way in your upbringing or schooling.

When I hear, 'They are much more intelligent than I am,' I wonder. 'Who are *they*?' This mysterious group is made of people who are never real, but who are shaping your life. You received this message in your past, from others, and assimilated the belief into your sense of self. You believe that it is true without question. On the day you adopted this belief, it started to shape your life. In time, it came to feel like it was a part of who you are.

Where does this idea come from? Intelligence is a huge and varied field. If you cannot read, but you have a way with animals that very few others have, are you not intelligent? If you have an interest in drawing and painting, but not in mathematics, does this make you less intelligent? If you are an aware, considerate mother to your children, does this not make you intelligent? Who made these rules? Who decided on who could pass as intelligent and who could not?

This simple belief (like many others) will have a huge effect on your life if you don't start examining it. You could discover, like many of us, that you, too, carry many beliefs that define you as generally not good enough. These beliefs are simply not true.

Questions to ask yourself
- What do you believe about yourself that may not be true?
- Which beliefs about yourself are worth a closer look?
- Which beliefs have you received that you believe are true, but may no longer be?
- What is really true about who and what you are? Who planted these ideas in you?

Most of us carry, believe and live the idea that we are not good enough. In therapy, when I ask the question 'When will you be good enough?', most people do not know when exactly they will step into that mysterious space called 'good enough'. If we were to reach that place, we still wouldn't feel good enough. It's like chasing a rainbow.

'Good enough' is an illusion. The truth is that it is impossible to feel good enough all the time – and it doesn't matter. Many of our other ideas, which influence our way of being and our experience of ourselves, do not exist either. Perfection does not exist. Low self-esteem does not exist. Somebody gave birth to it, and you adopted it. We have general ideas about, and language for, not being good enough, which do not make us feel better or help us.

Instead of seeking to be perfect, more intelligent or good enough, focus on speaking the truth about all the dimensions of yourself. To become brutally honest about who you are, you need to start the process of getting to know yourself.

You need to ask yourself what is really true for you. You are the author of your life. You need to update your own files and take a look at your truths.

Define yourself with awareness and truth

Self-awareness is about constantly seeking to see more of yourself in any context of your life. It is an essential part of being alive. It is a simple truth that you cannot love yourself if you do not know yourself. To know yourself, you need to take a closer look at who you really are.

To love yourself is to know yourself
Doubting and questioning yourself constantly is a sign of damage and disconnection. It is a sign that you are not being the person you should be, and that you are removed or disconnected from your truths. The damage that disconnects you from yourself can come from the relationships that surround you or from your relationship with yourself. Doubting yourself removes you from what is true about yourself. As a result, you will never feel good enough. If you are lost in a confusing mess of doubts, ask yourself what is really true.

Start seeing more of yourself

Instead of doubting yourself in ways that do not give you any answers, start facing yourself with complete honesty. This means that you need to stop running away from who you really are. Stop comforting yourself with food, sleep and substances. Comforting yourself is avoiding yourself, and the truth is that what feels comforting is not always good for you. End the avoidance and start the journey of getting to know the most important person in your life: you. When you stop avoiding and start having a closer look at yourself, you will end the doubts and questions about who you are. It is an exhausting waste of your life to live in doubt; it is a relief to see as much of yourself as you can with great honesty.

One simple way of starting to raise your awareness of yourself is to journal your thoughts and feelings. Writing down your innermost thoughts and feelings over time will start to reveal more of yourself.

Examine all the parts of your life. Look closely at your life choices, relationships and reactions in different situations. Keeping a record of your life (even for a short period) will give you a lot of insight into the person you really are.

Questions to ask yourself
- How do you react if you don't get what you want or need?
- How do you express yourself when you are upset, angry, disappointed or sad?
- How do your express yourself when you are happy or in a good mood?
- What upsets you? And how do you handle it?
- When do you feel joy?
- How do you react if you disagree with someone?

Invitation to yourself
Start making notes, today, about yourself in the life that you live. Keep documenting your experiences of life and yourself for at least 30 days, and see what you discover.

Speak the truth about who you really are

Living your truth starts with speaking the truth.

Becoming honest about who you are and defining yourself truthfully is not about positive self-talk. The message you may have received – that you need to have positive thoughts about who you are to make yourself feel better – may, indeed, make you feel better, but that feeling does not last.

Speaking the truth is not as simple as the idea of positive thinking. Many of the people I meet try to have more positive thoughts. Doing so might have a positive effect for a while, but it seems to fade quickly. The truth is that there is no point in having positive thoughts that you don't really believe.

So, instead of trying to speak positively, try to speak truthfully – about the good, the bad and the scary parts of who and what you really are. This means liberating yourself from the idea of being good, positive or perfect, and focusing on being as gently honest as you can be. You need to define yourself with honesty and not through perfection or goodness.

To love yourself is to speak the truth about who you are.

With speaking the truth comes relief. The relief tells you that you are on the road to a loving relationship with yourself. It is impossible to love who you are without first becoming honest about all the parts of you.

As in any relationship, what you say when you become honest is, initially, not easy to hear. In fact, it seems that the discomfort that comes with honesty is often the first step in the direction of getting comfortable and reconnecting with yourself. This discomfort with speaking the truth is also why we tend to avoid ourselves. Accept the discomfort as part of the process of honesty, and be reminded that your intention is to get real about who you are. Your journey to change and happiness starts with speaking the truth.

Knowing what is true about you will ground you like an anchor. What can you say about yourself with absolute certainty? You are grounded in your truths.

You also need to think about the person you would like to be. It is the person you will grow into if you start living truthfully.

What does it mean to speak about who you are? It means describing yourself in a way that you think is true. You could start with general, one-dimensional descriptions: 'I am stubborn and brave and honest …'

Take notes from the patterns that repeat themselves. Learning from every joyous and painful experience is the nature of life.

The truth about who you are lies not in what you have or what you do.

The experience of you is your truth.

What does define us is how we are with others and ourselves, which starts with being with ourselves. What we do to others, we do to ourselves. If you are judgmental of others, you are most likely doing the same to yourself, often in an amplified way; if someone is judgmental of you, know that this is also happening on the inside of that person.

People may not remember your name or what you were wearing when they met you, but if you bring honesty and a lightness of being, they remember that. The experience and energy of you are what matters most. The powerful boss with the bad attitude will be remembered more for his bad attitude than for his strong management skills. How you experience yourself and the people around you will give you a greater sense of your true nature. The experience and energy of you are what people remember, not what you do and have.

Intelligence, looks and status mean nothing if the experience and energy of you as a person are not good. That light that shines through your eyes, and not your suffering or your pain, is the person you are and the person with who others seek to connect. It is the person you know you really are.

Invitation to yourself
It is often difficult to know who you are. If you find it difficult to see yourself, ask someone you really trust to tell you how they perceive you. Do not accept every description of yourself as true, however. Decide for yourself which characteristics of your identity you know for sure are true. Nobody knows you as well as you do.

Start developing a new inner voice that is kind and gentle

When most people speak about themselves honestly, they tend to speak critically about themselves. Why, if you are being honest with yourself about who and what you are, do you need to be critical or reprimanding? Your intention is to be honest and not critical.

To love yourself is to speak about yourself with honesty and gentleness.

Learning a new, gentle way of speaking, one that takes care of you, does not happen overnight. Like growing a new, healthy habit, it is your constant reminder to be kinder and gentler in every inner interaction. Becoming kinder to yourself does not give you permission to let go of, or hide from, your responsibilities – it is an invitation to change the experience of yourself with honesty and gentleness.

We are beautiful human beings in our many 'imperfect' dimensions and layers. Our beauty lies in the richness of our dimensions and in our complexity. Therefore, when you speak the truth about who you are, it is essential to remember these truths about human nature:

You have many dimensions
Our beauty lies in our many dimensions. Like an artwork, city, song, book, or garden with layers of beauty, we have layers of dimensions.

Sometimes we are strong; sometimes we are weak. Sometimes we are beautiful; sometimes we are nasty. In certain situations, we are relaxed; in others, we are a mess. We are not one thing alone.

You cannot be generalised

Most people I meet speak about themselves in general terms. They say things like, 'I am really quite stupid', or, 'I am not that intelligent', or 'I am fat, ugly, insecure and neurotic.' Almost every person I have met has told me, 'I have low self-esteem.' Of course, we are all insecure or low on self-esteem in certain areas. Insecurity is part of what defines us as human. It does not make you 'not good enough': it makes you human. Insecurity comes from the expectation of perfection. The truth is that if you believe there is a perfect life for you, but that you are not living it, you will always feel insecure.

Human beings are not general. We are diverse and unique. Defining yourself with a generalising statement such as 'ugly and fat and stupid' does not reflect a truth. I do not believe in the language of low self-esteem, as it is too general and one-dimensional and only makes us all feel more worthless. Become interested in honest, interesting, multidimensional descriptions of yourself, which start with how you speak to yourself about yourself.

You are more than your body

In a world obsessed with looking good, we define ourselves by the look and shape of our bodies. Our bodies have an overpowering voice in our experience of ourselves. We use our bodies to rate and define ourselves as good enough, worthy and beautiful. We forget that many aspects of ourselves describe us as beautiful and worthy. We are much more than just a body, and should grow many descriptions of ourselves that are not about how we look. This does not mean that your body has no voice or doesn't matter – it simply means that your body should never be the dominant voice that describes you. What about your soul, spirit and energy?

You are energy

When you talk to someone or walk into a room, you bring energy with you. We are energy, and the memory of you is the energy of you. It is what you build your relationships on. A person who fits the mould for looking good, but has heavy and critical energy, is always less attractive. Inconsistent energy that moves between presence and absence is never a good experience. We are attracted to people's energy that feels honest and consistent. If you remind yourself about the importance of your energy as the experience of you, your need to be perfect or good enough will fall away.

You are not perfect

We all know that when it comes to human nature, perfection does not exist. Your 'perfection' lies in your honesty and awareness. It seems more important to have a meaningful, interesting and honest life than the lie of a perfect life. If you think the perfect life exists, you will live a life dominated by control and worry about what others think of you. Your life on social media will never be your real life. No one else is living your life, and control is not a way of being. You have to live your own life and make your own decisions.

Speak the truth about your 'imperfections'. Take responsibility for your own choices and their consequences by knowing them and being honest about them. You are supposed to make decisions that are not good for you, sometimes.

Your 'imperfection' is not a hiding place from which to be a bully or not to work on yourself. It is your life's work. Striving to be kinder, gentler, stronger, wiser and richer in experience is your focus. Your 'imperfections' are your invitations to learn and grow.

Confront and take responsibility for the parts of you that need some work. Stay conscious of how you can affect others and work on being an aware and responsible person. Instead of thinking of yourself as good or bad, or right or wrong, or perfect or imperfect, spend your energy on staying aware of yourself and speaking the truth with kindness.

In your striving for 'perfection', nothing will ever be good enough. There will always be something bigger or better. Striving for perfection is the birthplace of your critical, harsh, reprimanding voices. We have internalised an inner dialogue that criticises us to make us try to do better next time: 'That was okay, but it could have been better'; 'I should rather have …'; 'If only I had …'; 'What am I doing?'; 'Don't be stupid!'; 'I am such a fool!'

We are hard on ourselves, and constantly strive to be better and more perfect to the point of losing our internal gentleness and kindness. There is no point to speaking to yourself in general and critical ways. Your pursuit of perfection holds no meaning, and leads only to exhaustion.

Your work is to:
- become aware of your perfectionistic, generalising and critical inner voice; and …
- develop a new, loving voice once you start becoming aware of how you speak to yourself internally and what it is doing to you and your relationships.

2. CHANGE WHAT IS AROUND YOU

Often, the experience of you is determined not by what is in you, but what is around you. The experiences that you choose to have and the people you allow into your life have an effect on your experience of yourself and your life. If you don't feel good about who you are, consider looking not only at what is happening on the inside of you, but also what is around you. You become the experiences that surround you.

Looking at the outside of your life does not make others responsible for your unhappiness, or for changing your life. If you believe that your unhappiness is not your responsibility, but others' fault, you are not taking responsibility for your life. Stop blaming others for your unhappiness. You are responsible for what is around you. Instead of looking at what others can do to make you happy, look at what you need to do to have the life that you would prefer.

To love yourself means not waiting for others to change your life. It means taking charge of your happiness.

Carefully select every experience that you allow on the inside and the outside of your life. Experiences outside you that constantly confuse you and make you question and doubt yourself are not good for you. Doubt, confusion and questioning yourself constantly are signs that a person or relationship is, most likely, not taking care of you. Doubting yourself constantly removes you from what is true about yourself. If you are lost in a confusing mess of questions and doubts, ask yourself what is causing the chaos in your life.

To love yourself is to put the experiences that you do not want on the outside of your life.

People who are judgmental of who you are will never be your best friends. The people you allow into the space of your life determine the experience of your life. If the people around you are critical, dishonest or mean, it becomes impossible to love yourself.

Carefully select the people who make up the experiences of your life.

Without judgment, carefully choose the experiences with which you would prefer to surround yourself. Meaningful relationships are a source of richness and meaning. Real relationships add to your life – they do not upset or confuse you, and take nothing from you.

Your closest relationships should encourage you to be who and what you are, and not make you constantly doubtful or question yourself. Your closest relationships should be honest and kind, not critical and confusing. Your loved ones will be there consistently in good and bad times. Your best friends will show an interest and support for you, as you do in return.

To love yourself is to surround yourself with experiences you want.

Start recognising the experiences and people who negatively influence your life, and put them outside your life. How do you do this?

What is in the circle of your life is the experience of your life, and will shape how you feel about yourself. Look at how you can change the experiences of your life by moving in the opposite directions of what you do not want or by ending or taking a break from what is negative. You need to take space away from the people who do not enrich your life. Move them further away from the circle of your life by spending less time with them. This does not mean simply ending

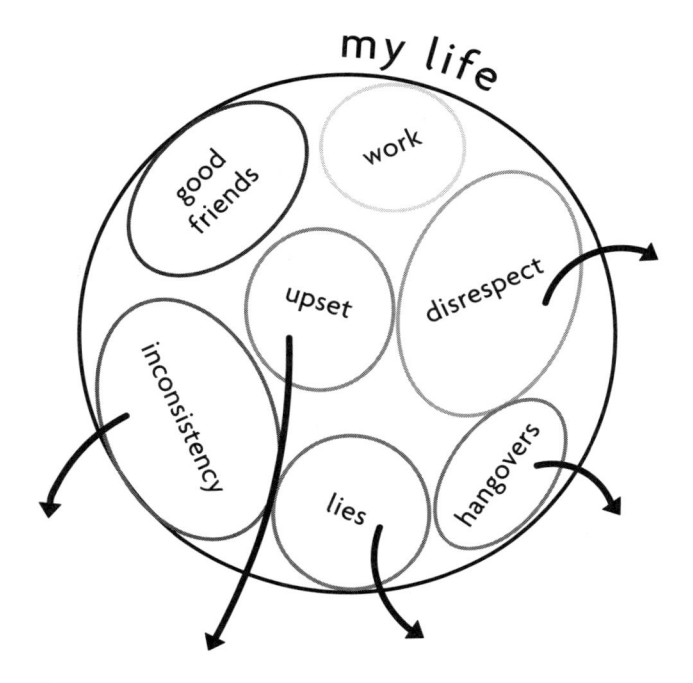

[Diagram: a circle labeled "my life" containing ovals: "good friends", "work", "upset", "disrespect", "inconsistency", "lies", "hangovers", with arrows pointing outward from several of them.]

all the relationships that do not take care of you: every relationship brings experiences that might matter to you in certain contexts. Don't simply throw out what you don't want, but slowly put it into a place in your life where it no longer hurts or upsets you. Sometimes, this means ending a relationship that no longer gives you anything of value. Moving away from people and experiences that do not take care of your life is called growth, but hold the ones who are consistently, honestly and respectfully in your life close and dear.

Surround yourself with people who see you accurately and accept you as you are.

Questions to ask yourself
- Which experiences in the circle of my life do not take care of me?
- Which experiences would I like to have more of, and would enrich and enhance my life?
- Who is causing upsets and chaos, and who is bringing love to my life?
- What is around me that upsets me constantly?
- Which people in my life show a real interest in who and what I am?
- Who loves and respects all parts of me?

3. LEARN TO COMFORT YOURSELF

When your best friend is beside you when you are upset and is gently comforting you, you need to learn to comfort yourself.

Comforting yourself during difficult times is a step into adulthood. Instead of leaning on others to make you feel better or to calm you down, you find your own ways of soothing and calming yourself. You are no longer the child looking to his or her parent for comforting words, but have learnt to speak gently and calmly to yourself in difficult times.

Not everything that feels comforting is good for you. Using substances and food to comfort yourself may initially feel comforting, but does not take care of you in the long run. When you feel triggered and your emotions are spinning out of control, it is especially important to find unique ways of soothing and comforting yourself. Like a parent who takes care of a child, you learn ways of 'parenting' yourself when you are hurting.

If you don't learn how to comfort yourself, you may always look to others to give you the calm you need. This could have an exhausting impact on your relationships and also cause you to run back to a relationship for comfort, even if that relationship has ended or is not good for you. If you do not know how to comfort yourself, you could hold on to relationships or struggle to end relationships that are clearly not taking care of you. You have to rely less on the people around you to always be there when you are in need, and find your own ways to peace and calmness.

Questions to ask yourself
- How can I comfort and soothe myself when I feel upset or hurt?
- Which of my ways of comforting myself do not take care of me?
- What is the best way for me to get to that place of calmness?

VISUALISATION
During a time of intense or out-of-control emotion, imagine one of your best friends standing next to you, gently and calmly speaking to and being with you. What is your friend saying and doing that calms and centres you? Apply those words and actions to yourself.

4. CHANGE WHAT YOU DO

Feeling stuck in a life that feels small and lonely, a life that bores and exhausts you and does not give your meaning and energy, is your invitation to make some changes. It is less in the talking than in the doing.

It is not in the talking but in the doing that you start changing.

You have a right and a responsibility to live a life you prefer. A life that enriches you with meaning and joy is the experience of a life that matters most.

As with your relationship with yourself, the life around you holds a richness and depth of experiences that only you can access. Pain is part of life, but life also holds so much beauty and joy – which is all around you.

If you are stuck in a comfort zone of parenthood, work and domestication, you need to make a change. If your life is about nothing more than work and watching television, your life is too small. If the pattern of your life is exhausting you, life is asking you to make a change. Constant exhaustion is your cue that you are not living your best life. Maybe your life has become too superficial, materialistic and one-dimensional. Maybe your life has become all about work and parenting. To enrich your life with meaning and experience, take any of the following steps:

Stop worrying about what people think of you

To choose the experiences that matter to you the most, you need to stop worrying about what others think of you. The life you prefer is not one that you've copied from someone else. To love yourself is not to worry what others think of you.

This does not mean that you do not care about others or yourself. It is about not giving people who do not really know you or care for you power over who you are. You need to know what is true and what is not true about yourself. As you cannot control what people say about you, all you can control is what you know is true about yourself. There is no point in trying to control how people perceive you. Instead of worrying about what people think of you, focus that energy on living a life that feels true and meaningful for you.

Questions to ask yourself
- How important are others' opinions of me?
- Why is it important to me what others think about me?
- How does this really impact on me?
- What can I do to be less affected by worrying about what others think?

Switch off the television

Although watching a lot of television can become a familiar, comforting space, it seems that life starts happening when you switch it off. Over time, watching television becomes a space of escape that holds less and less meaning. The perception that watching television programmes relaxes and energises you is not true in the long run.

switch off the tv

please

Invitation to yourself
Challenge yourself to an evening or day or week with no television and ask yourself how you could spend that time and energy in a more meaningful and enjoyable way. What are you missing out on while spending your life in front of your television?

Get to know your area

Your life may happen in your home, but there may be richness of life right where you live – you may just not know about it. Get out of your home and explore your neighbourhood, town or city and see what you would like to connect with.

Invitation to yourself
Identify an area that is close to you, in which you would like to adventure. Book a time to go there and look for places with good energy that speaks to you.

Be grateful for what you have

In our search for more, we overlook and forget what we have.

In our time-pressured pursuits, we lose perspective about what matters and what we should be grateful for. Gratitude means retaining perspective about the things you do have, the good and beautiful in your life. To live without gratitude is to lose perspective on life: you do not see what you have. The real gifts of life do not cost money and are all around you.

Invitation to yourself
For one week, remind yourself about, or write down, what you are grateful for. Do this in the morning or evening with consciousness, and see how it changes your experience of life.

Make some good memories

A life without constant good memories feels like a life not worth living. Do not wait for invitations from others to give you good memories. Actively create your own. A good memory, like a good story, adds dimensions to your life. The more beautiful memories you have, the richer the experience of your life.

Invitation to yourself
Think consciously about an experience that you would treasure, and make a plan to create it. If you want people to be part of the experience, invite them into the experience and create a new memory. Memories can fade, so consider keeping a record of them. A memory only holds richness if it can be remembered.

Change your physical space

Living and working in a space that reflects more of who you are is a form of taking care of yourself. Being in a physical space that reflects your identity sends messages to yourself about your truths. Your space should remind you about yourself, and invite you to relax, enjoy and be. Your relationship with your physical space is a reflection of your relationship with yourself. To change your space is to change yourself.

Surround yourself with the things you love and that speak of your identity.

Questions to ask yourself
▸ Which changes can I make to my space to reflect who I am?
▸ Which change to my space would make the biggest difference to the experience of my life?

Learn to deal with your moods and temper

Your moods and your temper are the thieves of your joy in and connection to life. They can dominate every experience and turn it into something negative. Learning to control and manage your temper and mood swings will drastically improve all of your relationships, including your relationship with yourself.

When you lose your temper, you disrespect yourself and the people around you.

Invitation to yourself
Keep a record of your temper and moods for one month. Every time you lose your temper or your mood fluctuates, write it down. In this way, you will start

seeing what causes your bad moods and loss of temper, and how they really affect your life. Make a decision about how you can change this, and take that step now. Find the source of your mood swings and loss of temper in you, and not in your relationship, and make a change for yourself.

Take charge of your depression or anxiety

Most of us will experience symptoms of depression or anxiety at some point in our lives. Some people experience depression or anxiety for the first time at a young age, often between the ages of 18 and 25. Most seem to miss these initial rounds of depression and anxiety. By the time you reach your forties and fifties, you will have established whether you are prone to anxiety or depression. Investigate your family history. If there are traces of anxiety or depression on your mother or father's side of the family, then you need to be honest with yourself about the possibility. Look at different treatment options and take charge of your symptoms. Depression and anxiety can have a powerful disabling effect on your relationship with yourself and on all aspects of your life. Take charge of it before it takes charge of you.

Questions to ask yourself
- Are there traces of depression or anxiety in my family history?
- Am I prone to anxiety or depression?
- How does my anxiety or depression really affect my life? What can I do about it?

Look at your hormone levels and thyroid function

An underactive thyroid and a hormone imbalance can have as powerful an effect on your mood as the chemical levels in your brain. If you struggle with motivation, energy, a low sex drive or a low mood, see you doctor, find the source of your symptoms and consider a course of treatment.

Laugh a little, or a lot

It is difficult to enjoy a good laugh in the company of judgment, but there is nothing better than having a good laugh with people who love each other. Being honest with yourself about who you are allows you to laugh at yourself. The acceptance that comes with the realisation that you are imperfect gives us permission to be human. We never laugh from the heart in the company of perfection and judgment. Laughing is a sign that that we are relaxed in a loving, kind space – that we are with our people.

Invitation to yourself
Think about the people and experiences that will make you laugh and invite them into your life.

Spend time in nature

Nature is our reminder that beauty, and forces greater than ourselves, exist. Sitting on a rock at the sea, and looking at the power of the waves and the vastness of the ocean can give us a sense of space that puts our lives in perspective. Nature is a source of energy and richness.

Invitation to yourself
Have a nature experience that is bigger than you. Identify a place in nature and spend some time there. Invite your favourite people to walk or sit with you in nature.

Keep a journal

Your last experience is only as rich as your ability to remember it. Keeping a journal is one way to remember and recognise the richness of your life. Reading back through the pages of your journal often gives you an awareness of your life.

Invitation to yourself
Keep a journal for 30 days and see what you get out of the process.

Breathe, sweat and move

Loving yourself is about taking care of your body.

Coming home after a day's work and sitting on your bed, waiting for that feeling of motivation to exercise to come over you is misguided. Feeling good about yourself often starts on the outside, and moves to the inside. Doing any form of activity that allows you to breathe, sweat or move will help you feel better. But to get that feeling, you need to get active.

Invitation to yourself
- Think about your preferred exercise.
- Decide when you can fit it into your weekly schedule.
- Commit and do. No analysis needed.

Eat good food

It goes without saying that if you put nutritious, healthy food into your body, you will feel better.

Questions to ask yourself
- Which foods would I like to eat more of that will make me feel healthy and energised?
- Which foods will give me more than they take?
- Which kinds of foods would a person who values and respects himself or herself eat?
- How can I eat better food every day?

Walk

Going for walks on your own and with your partner, friends or family has a wonderfully healing power. Walking is gentle, relaxing and reflective. Couples who walk and talk together often feel much happier than ones who don't.

Invitation to yourself
Identify a safe place where you would like to walk and decide if you want to walk on your own or with someone you love.

Drop a bad habit

Easier said than done ... Commit to changing at least one of your bad habits. All substances disconnect you from yourself and are reminders that you are not taking care. It is difficult to develop a gentle inner dialogue in the company of a bad habit. If you are stuck in a pattern that does not make you feel good about yourself, it needs to change. If you try to change it, but constantly break your agreements with yourself, then get some help.

Invitation to yourself
Decide on one bad habit that you would like to change and set yourself a goal. Decide for how many days (if not permanently) you would like to go without the bad habit, and feel the change.

Step outside the patterns of your every-day life

The pattern of work, meals, children, television, sleep and back to work does not always give our lives meaning. It is when you step outside the routines of your life that you will start feeling that you are living again.

Invitation to yourself
Choose one day per week when you allow yourself to do something that you don't normally do. Think of something that you always used to enjoy, but have neglected and would like to do more often. Then make a date or two to do it.

Get some sleep

The healing qualities of a good night's rest need no explanation. What feels big inside could have more perspective after some sleep. If you have problems with sleeping through the night, get some help.

Spend time in or near water

The healing qualities of water are well known. Spending time in or near water can shift and clear your energy.

Invitation to yourself
Choose a place where you can spend time in or near water, and feel the change.

Invite people into your life

Think of people whom you can invite into your life, then create experiences to share with them. Instead of waiting for others to change your life, create your own invitations. This will create new energy and opportunity. Every person is a network of possibilities.

Questions to ask yourself
- Who can I invite into my life?
- Which kind of invitations or experiences would I like to share with others?

Climb a mountain

Walking up a mountain is not only about spending time in nature and breathing some fresh air, but also reminds us that life can have uphill and beauty in the same space. The feeling of sitting at the top of a mountain and looking down at the view is priceless.

Invitation to yourself
Choose a mountain path and go for a hike. Take some friends or pets, and a treat for the top.

Step outside of time

If your every movement feels regulated by time, you can take care of yourself by stepping out of time when you get the chance. This means spending time not feeling rushed, time-conscious or limited by time. Taking your watch off for a day or two could help you to do this. The more time you give yourself or your relationship away from that constant, unhealthy awareness of time, the more you could start feeling connected to yourself.

Questions to ask yourself
- How can I (we) step away from time?
- How can I (we) create more spaces that are not regulated by time?

Listen to music

Instead of switching on the television, try listening to music. Music adds another dimension to anything you enjoy. It can enrich the experiences of walking, gardening, reading, cooking and whatever you love.

Invitation to yourself
Think about the music you love, or ask friends to make some recommendations. Fill you ears and your home with music while you enjoy the things you love.

Garden

Many people tell me how they find meaning and relaxation in gardening. Our relationship with plants and soil often gives us space for perspective. Like an active meditation, gardening is a healing space for many.

Invitation to yourself
Get some pot plants, or turn a small space into a living oasis.

Cook

Even if you believe you are not a good cook, the process of creating something from scratch and sharing the result can be very rewarding. Whether you follow a recipe or use your intuition, cooking can be reflective, healing and delicious.

Invitation to yourself
Choose a dish that you have always wanted to make. Find a recipe, and make it.

Read a good book

Books are a wonderful way to climb into another life. A good book reminds us of the importance of real people. Like the characters who grow on you, you are also full of dimensions and richness.

Invitation to yourself
Ask a friend or family member who knows you well which books they recommend, or hang out at your favourite bookshop and find a book that speaks to you. Switch off your television and start reading.

Surround yourself with creativity

From painting to drawing to taking photographs to simply walking through an exhibition, creativity can inspire and enrich your life. You don't have to be the creative one, but you can look for and explore the creativity of others that is all around you.

Invitation to yourself
- Think of a creative activity that will give you joy, and do it.
- Think of an exhibition in your area that you would like to see, and see it.

Slow down

Slowing down is about consciously focusing on taking your time and becoming aware of yourself and what you do. In a world in which every activity is measured by time, we disconnect from what we are doing and how it feels just to get it done. From cooking, eating, walking and talking, slowing it down may help you to see more of what you are doing and who you are.

Questions to ask yourself
- Which activities in my life would I like to slow down? Why?
- What do I connect with – in myself and in what I do – when I consciously slow down the process of doing things?

Be here, now

Being present in the now, and not always living in the past or worrying about the future, is a mindset and a way of living that will change the experience of your life.

Questions to ask yourself
- How can I be more present in what I do?

The list of simple actions that have big effects on your life and your relationship with yourself is endless. All of these actions share similar experiences. The steps you take to expand and enrich you life will also:
- re-energise you;
- make you feel alive and proud;
- give your life meaning and dimension;
- make your life more interesting;
- relax you; and
- give you enjoyment.

Your intention is to do what matters to you and what you know would give you great joy. There is no point in just talking about the changes you would like to make. You need to do what you say.

5. DO WHAT YOU SAY

Just as others can lie to and deceive you by not keeping their promises, we lose faith in ourselves when we don't stick to what we know and feel is good and right for us – when we break our own trust.

When you do what you say you are going to do, you step into the process of trusting yourself again. When we don't do what we say, it becomes difficult for us to trust ourselves – like that friend who makes empty promises but never delivers. Trusting yourself is about sticking to your own promises and commitments. The signs of losing trust in yourself include doubting your decisions and feeling out of tune with your intuition.

Loving yourself means doing what you say you are going to do.

To trust yourself again, you need to stick to the agreements and commitments that you set out for yourself. You need to switch on to your awareness and the inner voice that guides you during your most difficult decisions. Most of us have no problem with awareness. We can clearly see where we neglect and abandon our own decisions, when we do not take care of ourselves and when we do not listen to our intuition. We often have a strong awareness of what takes care of us and what does not. But why – if we have such awareness, if we know and can see what we are doing – do we repeat the same patterns?

It is true that you cannot change what you cannot see. But once you have seen and understood what you need to do, you need to move beyond awareness into a place of doing. Loving yourself at this point is more about doing than talking. Often, we don't trust ourselves enough to put our awareness of what we need to do into action. We hide behind our fear; it feels like we don't know what to do next, even if we do.

It is in the doing and not in the saying of what you have to do that your fears and insecurities will move into the background.

Therefore, trusting yourself is about listening to your feelings and thoughts, seeking to see and understand yourself, and then putting your knowledge about yourself into action. When you listening to your feelings and thoughts by acting upon them, you start trusting yourself. When your words and actions are one and the same, you start trusting again.

When I hear, 'I would like to start my own business, but I am too afraid', or, 'I would like to lose weight, but I don't feel confident enough', I am reminded that fear and confidence are not things that change your life. Awareness, truth and *actions* change who you are.

If you feel overweight and this is making you unhappy, decide which steps you can take to lose weight.

When people complain about their bodies during therapy, I find it interesting how we get stuck in self-analysis. We have examined ourselves from every angle and gained an in-depth understanding of our needs, what we should be doing and why we are not doing it. What is often needed is not more self-analysis, but a serious plan of action. As our bodies change shape and as our eyes start to shine again, we start to feel who we are supposed to be. It is in the doing that we start to feel better. You can still take action if you are afraid and have what feels like low confidence. Being fearless and confident is not a requirement for change. The truth is that fear and insecurity are essential for change.

Of course, you will make decisions that feel like mistakes, that cause shame and regret; decisions in which you can now see how you abandoned yourself. It was not your intention to neglect yourself – you made a decision based on what you thought would be best at the time. Every decision that causes upset, chaos and pain will direct and support you on your path to a greater sense of trust. It is when you make decisions that are not good for you that you get an opportunity to learn and become more aware. Each painful round teaches you more about what you don't want and where your preferred life lies. Upsets and pain are constant reminders of your truth.

Trusting yourself means feeling, with greater certainty, that you would make the right decision if you were put back in the same difficult situation. It means feeling secure in your ability to make good decisions that will take care of you. You will walk away with a sense of respect and integrity for yourself. Your words and actions will become the same.

Questions to ask yourself
- Which aspects of my life are not taking care of me?
- Where do I neglect and abandon myself?
- What would I like to do more of that would make me feel better about who I am?
- Which steps or actions can I take to trust myself again?

IN CLOSING

To love yourself is to:
- know yourself;
- speak the truth about who you really are;
- change the way in which you speak to yourself;
- speak to yourself with honesty and gentleness at the same time;
- develop a new inner voice that loves and takes care of you;
- put the experiences that you do not want to have outside your life;
- select the people who make up the experience of your life carefully;
- create your own happiness and not wait for others to change your life for you;
- surround yourself with the experiences you *do* want to have;
- expand and enrich your life; and
- do what you say (trust yourself again).

At the core of loving yourself is changing the way you speak to yourself about yourself and your life. Even if you fill your life with beautiful and enriching experiences, the experience of you and your life will never feel like love if you speak to yourself in harsh and critical ways.

If you feel overwhelmed and do not know where or how to start changing the experience of being you, decide on only one of the processes and put it into action. For example, making a conscious choice to speak the truth about who you are as often as you can will bring change. If you challenge and change your internal conversation and always try to be honest with, and kind to, yourself, you will start feeling a positive change.

Loving yourself is not about making one or two fleeting changes to feel better. It is a way of being that requires a new way of thinking. It is a lifestyle and a mindset. It is not a one-night stand with yourself, but a life-long interaction.

It is your life's work.

Chapter 8

ending a relationship

Most couples ignore their problems for a long time before they seek help. They believe that their problems will fix themselves in time, and ignore obvious signs. They live in various states of disconnection, hoping that things will get better. But time does not cause change – only working on your relationship does.

When it feels like your relationship is in a crisis and there is a threat that it might end, jump in and do some real work on it.

BEFORE YOU END YOUR RELATIONSHIP

Before you end a relationship, you need to ask yourself if you have done everything in your power to fix or save it. Ending a relationship without trying to make some real changes will cause you to repeat the same patterns in your next one.

A relationship crisis is an opportunity to work on the relationship. If you end your relationship without working on it first, it often feels like unfinished business. It leaves you wondering and filled with regret: 'If only I knew what I know now, we could have done things differently' or 'What if …?' This is why the threat of your relationship ending is an invitation to work on yourself and your relationship like never before. It is not the time to run away and avoid your problems; it is your time to do some work.

The idea that you both need to feel equally committed to each other to work on your relationship is not true. For most couples in crisis, one partner is often more committed to the relationship than the other. One partner is sure that he or she wants to be in the relationship, while the other is less certain. Certainty about wanting to stay together is not a requirement for doing some work. The fact that you feel uncertain about your relationship is a reflection of the crisis in which you have found yourself, and not a sign that it is over.

The truth is that you do not have to feel equally committed or certain about your relationship for a change to take place. What you do need is a commitment to doing the work, which needs to come from both partners. This means that you both have some hope left in you that your relationship might survive the crisis if you do make some changes. One partner might feel five percent hopeful, and the other 70 percent; one partner wants to save the relationship more than the other. As long as there is some hope and a willingness to work, your relationship stands a chance. Hope on its own is not enough.

You cannot build your relationship on hope for change alone. Hope is a good starting point, but means nothing without change. To increase your chances of saving your relationship, you need to move from hope into a space of action.

What are you going to do about it? What are you willing to try or change to save your relationship?

You do not need to feel very hopeful or certain that your relationship has a future to make changes. But you do need to accept the invitation caused by the crisis and decide which changes you are willing to make to yourself and your relationship. You need to give your relationship a chance to recover and repair itself for there to be any hope of change. To do this, you both need to do some work.

A real change

Change does not happen through words, but actions. Promises of change are empty if some real changes in behaviour do not follow them. And a real change is not just a 'guest appearance'. A real change is a consistent change in behaviour over time. It is a change that comes with an awareness of what you need to change and a deep understanding of how your past behaviour has affected others. Do not be fooled by empty promises, long explanations and apologies without awareness. When you look at your partner, who is promising not to do it again or take better care next time, ask him or her:

- What proof is there that you have changed?
- What are you working on and what are you trying to achieve?

Your partner's understanding of their behaviour, and your seeing this understanding being put into action over time, will give you some hope with substance. But a real change is not only about what your partner is doing for you – it is also what you are doing for them, and what you are doing together. A real change is a two-way street; one partner's problem needs both partners' participation. Therefore, the questions I often ask couples are:

What are you going to do from your side to contribute to the change? What is your responsibility?

What are you doing together to turn your relationship around? What is the responsibility of your relationship?

When you take action and start doing some work on your relationship, you will have clarity about your commitment. **Your willingness to try almost anything to save your relationship is your commitment.** During the work you do, you will start seeing where you both really are, and how committed – or uncommitted – you really are. Doing some work on your relationship starts with speaking the truth about what is really going on. And speaking the truth will open your eyes and show you where you really stand with each other.

The work you do on your relationship also has some risks. Speaking your truth is necessary for change, but it can be risky. As you work through the issues of your relationship, one or both of you may start to feel certain that you no longer want this relationship. You will start seeing your relationship and each other with the clarity that comes only through speaking the truth.

The answers to your questions will come when you work on your relationship.

The good news is that the work that most couples do increases hope, optimism and connection. They start to feel a greater sense of connection as they speak honestly, and they start seeing each other with greater clarity. The work often deepens their commitment. The harder they work, the better they feel.

Can our problem be resolved? What are our chances of fixing this problem? The truth is that you can work through almost any issue.

It may feel like hard work, but a break in trust or an absence of intimacy and sex can change. If you are constantly fighting, your relationship needs some new skills. You can even get your attraction back for each other and feel in love again if you are willing to work on your relationship.

The truth is that all you really need to solve your relationship's problems is the willingness of both parties to work on them. This means that the two of you are interested in making and willing to make some changes, no matter how you feel right now.

If your relationship is in crisis and in need of change, why would you not change it?

WHY RELATIONSHIPS END

To love someone is to treat him or her with respect; be honest and trustworthy; be kind and understanding; be responsible with your words and actions; and be interested in and willing to change.

When you partner tells you that they no longer love you, it means that you have lost one or more of the building blocks of your love. Trust, respect, attraction and interest are the experiences and actions of love. If you lose one or more of the building blocks of love, you start to question your feelings. It is difficult to love someone you no longer respect. For most people, it seems that losing two of the building blocks of love – respect and trust – changes your love. And the loss of three building blocks – respect, trust and attraction – often brings you to the relationship's end.

Most couples, however, do not end their relationships because they no longer love each other. They end their relationships despite still loving each other very much. I have heard, 'I love you, but I cannot be with you any longer' many times. The end of a relationship is seldom about a general loss of love, but about the loss of one or more of the building blocks of your relationship. Losing trust or respect for each other is enough of a reason to bring your relationship into crisis. If you have lost trust and respect for each other and refuse to work on it, it often signals the end of a relationship.

It makes no sense to stay in a relationship that feels damaging to you and shows no signs of change.

The most common reasons couples end their relationships are:
- how they speak to and treat each other;
- constant fighting and disagreement;
- a lack of emotional connection and understanding;
- a loss of trust;
- failure to prioritise the relationship;
- a loss of attraction;
- too many outside influences;
- addictions; and …
- differences in sexual preference and orientation.

How you speak to and treat each other

The damage that destroys our love for each other often lies in how we speak to or treat each other. The way in which you speak to and treat your partner holds the experiences of what we call love: 'If you love me, you will speak to me and treat me with respect.' If you promised each other that you would respect each other, but don't, you break the trust in your relationship. And the person who has no respect becomes less attractive over time.

So, how you speak to and treat each other holds three very important experiences of love: respect, trust and attraction. It is no wonder that this is one of the main reasons couples end their relationship. It is also one the areas that can change for the better if you are both willing to work on it. If one partner continues to treat the other badly and refuses to make changes, it gives you no hope.

Learning to speak to and treat people with respect is one of the sacred agreements of any relationship, and can be worked on.

Constant fighting and disagreement

If you do not learn how to resolve your differences, your relationship could end. Learning to disagree is a skill, and couples who often fight when they disagree could destroy their relationship.

For most people, the problem lies less in what you disagree about than in how you disagree. Learning to accept two opinions or perspectives in the same space, and that you both have the right to your positions, is surprisingly difficult for lots of couples.

Although any couple or person can learn to disagree, sometimes the fact that you cannot come to an agreement can mean the end. Even if you know that it can be okay to agree to disagree, sometimes not being able to reach an agreement can feel like a deal-breaker. Disagreeing about a point that feels so important to one or both of you that you would not be able to live with yourself if you were to give up your position can feel like the end. Important and sensitive areas, like having another child or parenting, can cause a disagreement that can end a relationship. For example, it seems important for most parents to be on the same page when it comes to how they parent or discipline their children. How you discipline your child reflects your own beliefs, your family history and your definitions of love, so it is difficult to agree to disagree about this.

Learning how to disagree without fighting is a skill that everyone should learn.

A lack of emotional connection and understanding

You can be seen and understood in all other areas of your relationship, but if you are not emotionally seen and understood, it feels like you do not really know each other. At the core of disconnection is emotional disconnection. In any relationship, it seems important to be emotionally understood, as it makes us feel not only seen, but loved. Being 'good with emotions' is not a requirement for seeing each other emotionally. All you really need is to see each other's hearts, souls and emotional insides, and to have an interest in, and a willingness to try.

An interest in each other's emotional words is a conscious mindset, and a skill that anyone can acquire.

A loss of trust

Most, if not all, couples experience a loss of trust at some point. This break in trust is not general, but specific: I don't trust you with my emotions, our finances, or speaking the truth about a specific area. A loss of trust is about not feeling safe or secure in your relationship in a specific area of your life. In time, a loss of trust in one area often becomes a general feeling of distrust.

Security and trust can be restored if both parties are willing to work on it.

Failure to prioritise your relationship

Couples who prioritise their work, children, interests, friends and family over their relationships could find their relationships in a place where they no longer have enough, or any, space in their lives. It is unrealistic to think that your relationship will always come first in all areas of your life. But a relationship that seldom or never receives priority over anything else in life cannot survive over time. It seems essential for the survival of any relationship that both partners sometimes need to give their relationship first place.

Prioritising your relationship over everything else in your life is your responsibility. Only you can give your relationship the first place it needs to survive.

A loss of attraction

A loss of attraction is often the reason couples end their relationship. Surprisingly, it is often not the loss of physical attraction that ends a relationship, but the loss of emotional attraction to each other. Emotional attraction is about how you speak to and treat people, your interest in each other's emotions and your control over your temper and moods. Physical or sexual attraction is about how you take care of your bodies, ageing, and what is happening in your intimate and sex lives. Getting stuck in patterns of too much domestication and administration is also not attractive.

Attraction is multidimensional and has to be worked on. If you don't feel attracted to each other, you can work on becoming more attractive to each other.

Too many outside influences

Too many influences from the outside can destroy the inside of your relationship. People and experiences that come into the space of your relationship can have such a strong influence on it that they change the experience of it. Often, these outside influences are beyond our control. Outside influences include traumatic events, interference from other people, too much work stress, depression and public attention. You may not have full control over outside influences because you did not invite them in, but you do have control over how you manage them in your relationship. A relationship without boundaries will get into trouble.

Setting boundaries for yourself and your relationship is a form of protecting your relationship, and a skill that anyone can learn.

Addictions

The destructive impact of any addiction on a relationship can empty out that relationship's essence. Sex, technology, food, television, gambling, porn, spending and drug addictions all have similar effects on a relationship. They affect the trust, respect and attraction you have for each other and often make it impossible to be in that relationship if things do not change.

Addictions need rehabilitation and can improve if they are worked on.

Different sexual preferences or orientations

Different sexual preferences or orientations are difficult or impossible to change. If your partner's sexual preferences are not in line with your identity and too much of a compromise for you, your relationship will end. Some couples find ways of working around these issues and can still co-habit and be friends and parents, but they often spell the end of your intimate relationship.

No matter how willing you are to work on your relationship and how much you love each other, certain issues are difficult or impossible to resolve.

ONE LAST CHANCE

What seems like the end of your relationship may not be the end. Sometimes, from the very edge of the end, couples have managed to turn their relationships around. The truth is that it takes one strong person to invite a relationship to turn around and give it one more chance. You *can* try to fight for your relationship. Without being desperate, you can take a strong stand that you do not accept the end of your relationship and, instead of letting go, speak up and encourage your partner to reconsider. You can invite him or her into the process of working on your relationship. Even from a place that feels like the end, you could start to see new growth.

If you have tried everything in your power to encourage the relationship to continue, however, and your partner still refuses to participate in it, you need to accept that there is nothing more you can do. If your invitations for change are met with a refusal to participate, you need to focus on letting go and taking care of yourself. The truth is that while one person can invite another to make a change, it takes two people to make the change.

THE END OF A RELATIONSHIP

If one partner wants to work on your relationship and the other does not, it is the end of your relationship. No matter what the issues are, if one or both parties are not willing to make changes, then you have to focus on letting go and accepting the end of your relationship.

Yet even when we know it is over, we hold on, despite having received the message very clearly. You might wonder: why do you go back or hold on when it is over?

Why do we keep going back?

To leave with a good impression of ourselves
The way we behave during a break-up often becomes the reason that we struggle to let go. Holding on when you have clearly got the message, more than once, that it is over, may fill you with shame later.

If you acted in a way that makes you feel ashamed, or that does not reflect who you really are or how you would like to be perceived, you might feel an inclination to go back for just one more round: 'I am sorry I acted so crazily, but I was really upset. I am really a nice, sane person.'

You could find yourself in a pattern of making contact that starts off very friendly, but ends up getting heated when you don't get the response you want. Often, we want to leave the best version of ourselves behind. If you have said things you regret, or behaved in way that embarrassed you, you may want to go back and clear your name.

Does it really matter? The best thing you can do to restore your self-worth is to turn your back and walk away.

The rejection and abandonment are overwhelming

The end of a relationship often leaves one partner feeling rejected and abandoned, powerful triggers that make us feel out of control. Emotional triggers are often layered with memories. When a relationship ends and you feel rejected or abandoned, your emotional memories of past rejection come to the surface. You find yourself dealing not only with the end of your relationship, but with your memories. This can be overwhelming and spin you out of control.

When we feel triggered, we feel such intense pain and fear that we lose control of our emotions and don't feel and behave like our 'usual selves'. The pain of the trigger also pushes us to try, desperately, to go back to avoid the pain. You need to recognise your rejection and abandonment triggers and work on them instead of looking to your past relationship for relief. The peace of mind you are looking for is in you, not in your ex-partner.

For our children and family

Often, we go back to a relationship for our children, to restore that sense of family. Your belief that a 'complete family' includes both parents might cause you to stay for the sake of your children, even if your relationship is in pieces. This is often a conscious sacrifice of your needs for your children's peace of mind. Of course, this path resolves nothing and makes nobody happy. And if you stay in destructive circumstances for the sake of your children, you damage not only yourself, but also your children. It is a difficult and complicated decision.

The hope for change
Sometimes we go back because we believe that this time things will be different. You may build that hope on little signs of warmth and love, instead of listening to the truth: that it is over. You may even receive promises of change. But change lies not in words – it lies in a change of behaviour over time. Hope can keep you in a situation that is not good for you. Rather look at what is real than colour things with your desires.

For the sex and intimacy
Sometimes, the sex and intimacy in a relationship can have such a powerful binding force that we stay because 'the sex is good'. Great sex keeps us going back as it creates the illusion of hope. The truth is that no relationship can last on a powerful intimate or sexual connection alone. And divorcing sex from all other parts of a real relationship is destructive.

If only I had another chance ...
Many of us go back because we believe in the potential of our relationship. You believe that if you had one more chance to show yourself and the relationship what you can offer, you could turn it around. You go back to the potential of what could be, instead of looking at what you really have. People who hold on often believe that they can rescue, change or save their partners. You might also believe that if you give more, you will get more. But these beliefs are all untrue – they are statements of denial. In simple terms, you are lying to yourself, which will keep you going back for more hurt. Rather focus on saving and rescuing yourself, and on letting go.

THE END IS THE END

We receive a lot of messages about how to find a partner, but seldom hear how to handle the end of a relationship. No wonder we feel so lost and confused during a break-up.

People send us messages like 'time heals all wounds' and 'this, too, will pass' at a time when your heart is broken and all you want to do is scream obscenities back at them! They neither make us feel better nor take the pain away. This is why we often go into hiding after a break-up. We avoid the happy couples, romantic movies and superficial advice. We go home, and lick our wounds, and cry – in private.

And that is exactly what you need to do. Confront the pain, focus on letting go of what was or could have been, and focus on your self. It is time to take better care of yourself than ever before. But what does it mean to confront your pain, let go and focus on yourself? This is what many others do when their hearts are broken:

End all contact

To move forward, you need a period of no contact with your ex-partner. As difficult as this can be, it seems that making contact or spying on social media when it is over can keep you emotionally hooked in, instead of encouraging you to let go. For peace of mind, end all contact: every interaction could trigger your feelings of rejection and abandonment. Avoiding constant upsets and triggers and focusing only on what you feel helps you to move forward emotionally. But if you keep opening what is closed, you stay in cycles of pain.

Do not judge or punish yourself if you relapse and make contact, as every round of upsets teaches you not to make contact again.

Remember that the end of your relationship also means the end of what you no longer wanted in your life. As painful as it can be, it is also the end of what caused you the pain of being in the relationship.

What happens at the end of your relationship is often a reflection of what happed in the course of your relationship. How you were treated by your partner and how you both behaved during your relationship will reveal itself in a more exaggerated form when the relationship ends. What didn't work for you in the relationship will show itself during your separation or break-up.

Stop avoiding your emotions

It is natural that when you are hurt, upset, or in pain, you just want to avoid how you feel and run away from your emotions. But your emotions only start changing if you confront them and speak the truth about them. Like a little dog trying desperately to get your attention when ignored, and barking more and more loudly until it does get your attention, your emotions need to be acknowledged. You then need to spend some time with your emotions to calm them down. Acknowledging and spending time with your emotions means asking yourself how you really feel, speaking honestly and openly about your feelings, and not trying to change them. Your emotions cannot be fixed. They simply need to be seen and acknowledged for what they are.

The end of a relationship could mean the loss of more than one person. You may lose friends or even family in the process. As with any loss, your emotions will move between sadness, anger, denial and acceptance; and, as with any grief, we need to acknowledge what we feel to move forward.

Stop the blame

It is easy to get stuck in a cycle of blame and finger-pointing. If you point a finger at your ex-partner alone, you may not have looked at your part in the break-up. Speaking the truth to yourself about your own responsibilities and those of your ex is a step in the right direction. As painful as it can be to see your part in the breakdown of your relationship, it could also feel hugely liberating to speak the truth and claim some responsibility. People who blame their ex for their break-ups never really move forward, and stay stuck in the same story of blame.

Comfort yourself

Imagine your best friend standing next to you, speaking kindly to you and comforting you when you are in pain. This is how you comfort yourself. Speak to yourself in kind and gentle ways, and do not judge or criticise yourself for what has happened. The end of a relationship is the time to take better care of yourself. From eating good food, to exercising, to sleeping, you need to do what makes you feel better during this painful time.

Remember what is true about you

The experience of a relationship ending often confuses our sense of self. We no longer know who we really are. To get your strength back, you need to remind yourself what is true about you. Think about the parts of yourself that you neglected and compromised in your relationship, and take back what is true about you. You do not have to be defined by the end of your relationship.

Seek the company of friends and family

You friends and family may be tired of hearing about your former relationship, as you may have shared many stories about who did what in the run-up to the break-up. You may feel that you do not want to burden your friends and family with your pain, but this is the time to ask for help and support from the people you love. This does not always mean sharing and talking about your pain, but rather just being in the company of people who really love you and who make you feel better. It reminds you that you are loved.

Try to make sense of what has happened

You may feel that you need to make sense of every part of the end of your relationship to let it go. But doing so requires both of you to share your side of what happened and why. Because you ex-partner is, most likely, not interested in giving you that closure, and you are not speaking to each other anyway, it seems important to take charge of your own process to make sense of things. You probably have many questions without answers. Instead of digging deeper, focus on what you do know with certainty and come up with your own conclusions and understandings about what happened. You may have to accept that you will never fully understand what has happened.

Take your pain to nature

As oversimplified as it may seem, many have found that spending time in nature when their hearts are broken offers some kind of relief. Nature often reminds us that there are forces bigger than ourselves, which puts our pain into perspective. We are reminded that the pain we feel is part of a much bigger picture.

Get out

There is a slippery slope into that dark space of going into hiding. If you hide away and refuse to see friends and family, you could find yourself feeling depressed very soon. Even if you do not feel like it, take a step into the outside world.

Seek some help

If the end of your relationship overwhelms you to the point of not being able to function in your every-day life, or if you feel too down to work and be with people, you need to seek professional help. Finding the right therapist at this time can be very healing.

IN CLOSING

The middle of a break-up, when you heart is sore, is no time to be learning lessons. It is a time to take care of yourself and process your emotions. But if you paid the price of pain, you will hopefully find some valuable lessons further along the road to recovery.

Months – or even years – after a break-up, you may look back and pick up some **valuable life lessons**, like the ones that follow, that you can use in your next relationship experience or to help a friend with a broken heart:

The pain you feel will not go away until you face it. Time does not heal all wounds. Only an honest meeting with your feelings will ease your pain. Avoiding your pain will make it worse. So, whereas it is difficult to feel hurt, sad, angry and upset, you need to acknowledge what you feel and spend some time with your emotions before you can feel better.

Unprocessed emotion will follow you and surface in different shapes and forms in new relationships. If you avoid your pain, you will carry it for months or years.

You cannot allow yourself just to sit in your pain. You need to set a time frame for allowing yourself to feel what you are feeling. The space in which you allow yourself to feel what you are feeling needs to be a safe and gentle one. What you open, you need to pack away again, then continue living your life to the best of your ability.

How you deal with your break-up will determine the kind of relationship that you will have with each other in the future. If you still need to co-parent or want to remain friends, you need to remain respectful of each other during this difficult time. What happened in your break-up will shape your future relationships. How you treat each other in your break-up will set the tone for any future interaction.

A break-up is the end of what you didn't want. It is the end of all the behaviours and patterns that hurt you when you were in the relationship. This is why you may feel a mixture of relief and loss.

You cannot move forward if you do not acknowledge your part in the breakdown of your relationship. Even if your partner contributed a bigger portion of the damage, you still need to look at your part. People who always point a finger at others will never be free of their pain. When you speak the truth about your part in the breakdown of your relationship, you will move towards a place of peace.

The end of a relationship is not always the end. Sometimes, it is a change in roles. If you have children together, in particular, you will always be relating to each other, just in different or new roles.

The end of a relationship is always two people's responsibility. It is never a rejection of one partner by another, as you both share in the responsibility of where you are. What you have allowed and what you have done is always a two-way street.

You do not need to be defined by your break-up.

Your behaviour and needs in your next relationship will be defined by the wounds from your past relationship. We often look, in our next relationships, for what we didn't receive in our previous ones.

Your break-up does not have to be a rejection experience.

Every relationship is your opportunity to learn. When the pain has passed, use the opportunity to take note and absorb some relationship lessons so that you can move closer to what you really want in your next relationship.

If you find yourself repeating the same pattern, or sitting with the same problems in every new relationship, you need to take some time to make sense of why the pattern repeats itself. If you do not take note of what every relationship is trying to teach you, you will miss the opportunity for a more rewarding relationship in the future.

Being on your own after a break-up, instead of quickly moving on to your next relationship, is responsible. Carrying your pain into your new relationship could intensify your feelings. Because your need to feel better is driving you, you may think you are in love when you actually just need to feel better.

A relationship that starts with neediness instead of real interest and attraction always ends in tears.

epilogue

We seem to focus so much on why relationships end – but maybe the answers lie in why we start relationships … and how we take of each other along the way. The truth is this: the reasons that relationships end ultimately lie in the life of a relationship, rather than in the end of its life.

To be delusional is to have false ideas about the truth. In all of our relationships, we use our thoughts and not our experiences to avoid or change the reality or truths of our relationships. In other words, we wrap our relationships in beautiful wrapping instead of looking at what is really inside. Often, we believe the images we project on social media to be truths about our lives, but they are just our real lives' pretty packaging.

In our desperate need to be in a relationship and to share our lives, we adjust our own truths for the sake of love. We make excuses for damaging behaviour and we use our minds to override our emotions to stay in relationships. We believe our delusions, because the truth might change it all. And we build our relationships on the fantasy of what could be, instead of on the reality of what we have.

To move away from your delusions and fabrications, you need to look at what is true. The truth about your relationship is not in the pictures, but in the experiences of your relationship … and the 'experience' of your relationship simply equates to what it feels like to be in it. This is the experience that guides you towards your truth. If your relationship constantly confuses you, stresses you, makes you question yourself, or hurts you, you need to ask yourself: what is making me feel like this? *What is this feeling really doing to me?*

The process of listening to yourself will guide you into a space of truth.

I also had to learn truths about relationships. I had to learn to control my temper, and to speak in non-damaging ways. I broke and had to restore trust, and I had to find ways to comfort myself when my heart felt broken. I live with my pain and regrets with gratitude – because this book also comes from them.

Of course, it is not easy to see the truth. Once you see what is really going on in your relationship, it is often difficult to pretend that you have not caught a glimpse of its true face. But it is the beginning of change.

Chapter 9

questions and answers

My friends often joke that psychologists answer questions with questions, and that they walk away from them without ever really getting an answer to their questions. I find good questions with answers very useful, so this chapter may change your perceptions of psychologists.

It is with great caution that I provide general answers to general questions. In no way am I comfortable being the expert on someone else's life or relationship. It really is true that if you listen to and connect with yourself, you will find all the answers. I also believe in **getting honest with yourself, as you know yourself best**.

My intention is to draw from others' life lessons and my own experiences, and to share some of my observations as answers. I hope they give you some direction, insight and awareness.

TRUST

Q: *How is it possible for my partner to say he loves me, then cheat on me?*
A: It is difficult to understand why someone who loves you would cheat on you. Cheating and lying are not actions based on love, and we take it personally when our partners cheat on us. But people do not always cheat because of a lack of love. Cheating often says more about the person who cheats than your love for each other. The person who cheats is a person in crisis, and could be cheating because of:
- ego, selfishness or narcissism;
- loss of attraction due to ageing;
- loneliness and self-neglect;

- insecurity;
- depression;
- sexual dysfunction or addiction;
- long-standing problems with honesty, lies, deceit; or
- emotional unawareness, poor communication and immaturity.

The person who cheats might well need the safety and stability of a partner or family to cheat. If you remove the security of their relationship, their need for cheating falls away.

On the other hand, sometimes cheating does say something about your relationship. Cheating can speak of:
- loneliness;
- emotional isolation and disconnection;
- abuse (verbal, substance, etc);
- lack of communication and connection;
- boredom or too much routine; and …
- loss of attraction.

If the cheating is about your relationship, you will both have to work on your relationship and yourselves. As you can see, cheating is a complicated and multidimensional issue that goes far beyond love.

Q: *When do we lose trust? How do we know that trust can be repaired?*
A: A break in trust is a break in the spoken or unspoken agreements of your relationship. You may have certain expectations or understandings about which you know, or assume, you are in agreement. The most obvious agreement is that you will not cheat, or pursue another person for intimacy and sex. Even this most basic agreement has different interpretations. Some believe that sharing personal information, or information about their emotions, with someone outside their relationship is still within their agreement. Others believe that flirting is acceptable as long as it does not lead to sex.

You can see why trust is easily lost or broken. But trust is more often lost in the smaller, better-known expectations and needs in a relationship: you will not share that story I told you with my mother; you will speak to me with respect; you will not lie to me. Trust can almost always be repaired, as long as both of you are willing to work at it and neither of you repeat the pattern. You can only repair trust once or twice. If you give your relationship another chance, do not mess it up.

SEX AND INTIMACY

Q: *How important is sex with a life partner? Could one say that 80 percent is companionship and 20 percent is sexual?*
A: Your attraction to each other will increase and decrease as you move through life. It is the nature of relationships for us to move through different stages at different times, and to have different sets of needs during these stages. Sometimes sex will be more important than companionship; at other times, your attraction will be stronger. You need to stay aware of where you stand with each other throughout the life of your relationship to make sure that you know what you need from each other and your relationship. As you get older, companionship may become more important than sex. In my experience, happy couples have a comfortable balance of sex and attraction with companionship. Depending on the phase of your life, you need to ask yourself whether you can both accept this balance or imbalance of sex and companionship.

Q: *How is it possible that, as a couple, we can feel and be so intimate, but not have sex?*
A: The pathways to and energy of intimacy can be very different from the pathways to sex. Couples who share experiences, touch each other and communicate well can feel intimately connected, but might not feel like having sex with each other. You may recognise that you are very close in your every-day interactions, but feel neither the need nor the desire for sex. The closeness that comes with intimacy can often creates such a comfortable space that you feel like two friends who live together well. That comfort zone is not always the place from which sex happens. To connect sexually, you need to switch on to your bodies, your sexual minds, your desires and your wishes. You need to be apart to create a longing or desire for each other. For most couples,

stepping out of that space of intimate friendship into a space of sexual love often requires stepping outside their comfort zone.

Q: *How does one grow a relationship without intimacy and sex? Is this possible?*
A: A relationship without sex and intimacy seldom lasts in the long term, and there are many reasons. Many relationships can survive on intimacy without sex, but the experience of being touched and desired seems to be a very important part of being in a loving relationship. A relationship without sex and intimacy misses out on one of the most important pathways to connection and feeling loved. It is our basic human need to be desired, acknowledged and touched. When sex and intimacy are not present in a relationship (even if you accept that they are not), it often affects your sense of self. We start asking why we are not being touched, desired and wanted, which brings us to place of doubt in which we wonder whether we are loved. For this reason, a relationship without sex and intimacy may have difficulty growing, as it misses out on beautiful opportunities for closeness. Why would you accept this if you can have so much more?

Q: *We are always tired and never have energy or time for sex. How can we change this?*
A: If this is your problem, do not focus on sex as the solution. Rather focus on resting and relaxing. The more relaxed and energised you feel, the stronger the likelihood of sex. Not having time for sex is an excuse, because we always make time for what matters to us.

DISAGREEMENT

Q: *Could someone with a personality type that continually pushes, pulls, sabotages or taunts eventually provoke their partner to react and respond in a way that is out of character? Is an individual* **always** *responsible for their reactions; could there be a tipping point at which one responds atypically?*
A: Of course, it is difficult to remain calm and respectful if you feel constantly provoked. It is very difficult not to become a reaction to

each other's reactions, and not to respond in a way that is out of character in moments of conflict. But nothing justifies a reaction; you are always responsible for your own reactions. Becoming reactive always increases levels of destruction. If you feel provoked beyond a point that is reasonable, remain silent or walk away. Removing yourself physically is often the best step you can take. If this is the experience of your relationship, your relationship needs some guidance to end this damaging pattern.

DATING

Q: *Do you think we confuse being in love with being in lust?*
A: The idea and experience of being in love seems to be confused with many other experiences. The question I often wonder about is: with what did you fall in love? Being hugely attracted to someone – in lust – often intensifies our feelings for each other, making us think we are in love. Being in love often becomes about being hugely attracted to parts of someone, or in desperate need of what someone can offer. This person has qualities I like and need desperately – being together will make me better, younger and more beautiful, and give me a better life and sense of self. It is no wonder that the experience of being in love can fade so quickly, as it is not built on a real experience of love. Once you have got what you need, the relationship becomes real. We are often blinded by our desperate needs.

Q: *Why am I always attracted to people whom I know are intellectually unsuitable, but who seem to draw me in emotionally?*
A: You can clearly see that you have a pattern that repeats itself. A pattern is a recurring repetitive experience that becomes familiar over time, but does not change. If you can see that you are dating people you find emotionally attractive, but are not intellectually suitable, ask yourself:
- How can I recognise intellectual incompatibility sooner?
- What are the signs and symptoms of that intellectual disconnection?
- Most importantly, how can I turn away from what I do not want?

Your work is not about a lack of awareness. You seem to have no problem with seeing and describing the pattern of your relationships. You may need to look at why, if you can see what you don't like, you do not walk away. You might be building a relationship on its potential and not on the reality of what you see. You may be the eternal rescuer who believes that if you give a person the right kind of environment, exposure, respect, or love, he or she will grow into the person you need. But all you have is what you have right now. You cannot stay in a relationship based on only its potential.

Q: *I have been diagnosed with HIV. I live a healthy life on my medication and accept most aspects of life with a chronic disease. How do I process this internally and ensure that my old habits of seeing myself as worthless because of my status do not become such an overpowering force that I deny myself potential relationships before they start?*
A: You have a say in where you put HIV in your life. Even though it may always be part of you, you can decide on how much of a voice, and which place, HIV needs to have in your life. HIV does not define anyone as worthless – we give HIV that influence over us. Because of the unfortunate stigma attached to HIV and other chronic diseases, it is difficult not to get overpowered by the voices of 'others' who define you as less worthy. You need to see yourself – and your potential partner will have to see you, and not your HIV – as a definition or experience of you. Take back what is true about and important to you, and do not accept less than you are worth. Do not allow the voice of HIV to become your voice. Live your life from a place of what is really true.

Q: *The challenge of our generation is to develop a modern interpretation of how relationships work and to change the way we view relationships, which have become unrecognisable since the days of our grandparents. Which paradigm would you propose?*
A: Our parents' and grandparents' relationship paradigms have changed. In previous generations, women were discouraged from expressing their needs and opinions, and men were discouraged from expressing their emotions.

Yet, these relationship blueprints are still deeply engrained in many societies. They play out in our expectations of each other. When couples are stressed, in crisis, or disagree strongly, these deep-seated beliefs come to the surface. Women are still expected to defer to the needs of others, and men still believe their positions are 'more right'.

It takes time, in any new relationship, for these beliefs to surface. When you enter a relationship, it is important to look at how you behave and not at what you say. Often, I hear things like, 'I believe that men and women have an equal say,' but when it comes to making a decision, actions do not match those words.

I encourage people to speak about what they believe about relationships, and to be honest with each other. The paradigm of 'the truth about relationships' encourages both parties to speak honestly about their needs, thoughts and emotions to remain connected throughout the life of their relationship.

Q: *I keep dating partners who are unavailable. I recognise that this pattern is destructive, but struggle to break it. Why do you think I keep repeating the same pattern?*

A: I'm relieved to hear that you can recognise that dating unavailable partners is destructive for you. But it seems that your awareness of this pattern and the destruction it causes is not assisting you to break the pattern. People in faraway places, who have recently become single, or who are going through a major transition or crisis may not be ready or available for a relationship. Your work lies not in the pattern of your relationships, but in you. You need to ask yourself: why, if I can see that this person is unavailable, do I continue my pursuit? Why do I hold on when I can already predict the outcome?

It could be that your desperate need to be loved or to be in a relationship overpowers your awareness. If this is true, you need to work on yourself before you enter a relationship. Entering relationships with unavailable partners will hurt you and fuel your desperate need to hold on instead of letting it go. You need to learn to comfort yourself when you feel lonely or upset, and you need to start loving your own company.

CONDITIONS

Q: *Is narcissism a real problem, or is an individual who has narcissistic characteristics perhaps only displaying them to a particular partner because of that relationship's dynamic? Or will this individual continue to behave in that way in other relationships?*

A: Narcissism is a real diagnostic condition. Whereas lots of people have narcissistic traits, like being egotistical, self-absorbed and selfish, not all of them have a narcissistic personality disorder. In a world of selfies and reality shows, narcissism has become the norm.

The narcissist is a person with an exaggerated sense of self-importance. They believe they are better than others and should be treated differently. Looking good is very important; they tend to obsess about their appearance, as it is one of their most important tools for gaining the approval of others. They make good first impressions and present themselves with exceptionally good social skills, compliments and charm. But their self-absorbed and egotistical ways will show themselves in time.

Narcissists present themselves well for self-gain, but do not really feel the depth and intensity of emotions that others do. Relationships are there for them to receive, and are not opportunities to give. If they don't get what they believe they deserve, they respond with rage and indignation (called the narcissistic rage). They often hurt and upset others with their self-righteous ways, but move on quickly. This is why they often don't have many real friends, as their relationships are superficial and only relevant if they are beneficial on some level.

However, the label or diagnosis is not as important as the real impact of the behaviour. It is difficult – if not impossible – to be in a relationship where one person is always 'more right' and your needs are always less important. That is why the narcissist loves to date a 'pleaser', someone who loves to give more than they receive.

Pleasers also give more as they receive increasingly less, which is exactly the kind of relationship that the narcissist (and the pleaser) needs. When you realise you are not getting enough of what you need, and move into a space of disagreement, your relationship will quickly move into a crisis.

Even if narcissism can mellow with age, the prognosis is not very good. Rarely does the narcissist go for therapy to change their destructive ways.

Q: *I've been researching narcissism and sociopathic dynamics in relationships. Many people believe that they have fallen 'victim' to sociopaths, narcissists and even psychopaths, but are actually just creating problems for every solution because the drama seems to work for them. The cycle of charming, manipulating, demeaning and then discarding a romantic partner seems to resonate with many of the people who have experienced this sort of thing. Is this a legitimate problem?*
A: It seems that everyone who lies or cheats these days is suddenly a 'sociopath, psychopath or narcissist'. These are serious medical conditions that require a proper intervention. A personality disorder is a long-standing and destructive pattern, and not a reaction to a partner or a one-off appearance. If you partner has cheated or lied, it does not mean that they are a sociopath, psychopath or narcissist. The picture is much more complicated, and will have a long history of damage over time.

CHANGE AND GROWTH

Q: *Is it okay to change yourself quite substantially to keep a peaceful home and happy marriage, if you don't feel like it's destroying your soul? I have, somehow, always believed that if you couldn't be 100 percent yourself the relationship was not healthy. But I don't think I see it that way anymore.*
A: A relationship has an inevitable impact on both partners, and you should expect changes from both sides. What you need a relationship to be is an extension or expression of who you are. A relationship involves not only the expression of your own needs – you also have to yield to the needs of your partner. Your partner's needs may not always be as interesting, important and relevant to you as your needs, but they still require attention, consideration and participation. If participating in balancing each other's needs is not 'destroying your

soul', then doing so does not compromise your identity and can be perfectly healthy. A healthy, happy relationship requires you both to know what you need for yourselves and your relationship and the ability to share in each other's different needs without compromising your identities.

Q: *My husband has a pattern of not acknowledging his own feelings or those of others. Will he continue to repeat his actions in the future? How do I get him to acknowledge feelings?*
A: You cannot change something if you do not see or acknowledge it yourself, have a willingness to change it, or have an interest in changing it. You may have observed your husband's pattern of not acknowledging feelings, but he needs to start seeing it in himself. You can try to get him to see what you see by sharing your observations and asking him to work on this pattern.

This is an emotional invitation to change. It is like holding a mirror up to someone. Every time you feel he is not acknowledging your emotions, point it out to him or share your experience of him. Most people's first response to your holding up that mirror and pointing out their behaviour is defensiveness. You should expect this, but keep naming the behaviour that upsets you. Point it out from a place of love and concern and invite him to consider a change. That is the best you can do. If he refuses to see a pattern that affects you, it will repeat itself and you will be in a relationship that avoids communication. You need to ask yourself if you can live with this if no change takes place. Or you can insist on seeking help from a good couples therapist.

Q: *My partner is resistant to change. What can I do about it?*
A: There are many reasons for this. Resisting change can be about hiding behind traditional beliefs that support the position of being right all the time, refusing to accept different views, or fear of change. This traditional role delivers messages that are something in the line of, 'You need to like me as I am, otherwise you don't really love me,' 'This is me, love me or leave me,' or 'I am too old to change.' Excuses for not making changes often speak of fear – a fear of not knowing how to be different or how to change.

If you gently invite your partner to join you on a new and better path and extend an invitation to change with kindness and love, but are met with stubborn refusal, you have two options. You can try to speak about what the resistance is about, the reasons for possible fears, and what the resistance to change is doing to your relationship, or you can look at how committed your both really are. A refusal to change and move with each other often speaks of a lack of commitment to your relationship. At the heart of the commitment of your relationship is your willingness to grow, learn and move together.

A person who is not interested in your inner thoughts and feelings is not interested in or ready for you and your relationship. Interest and participation are required to dissolve the tension in your relationship.

Q: *What do you do when you believe that communication in a relationship is a good thing, but your partner avoids communicating to solve issues in your relationship?*

A: Even if you avoid communication, I think we can all accept that regular communication is essential for any successful relationship. For many, communication has negative associations. 'Can we talk?' or 'I need to talk to you' will cause resistance if talking always leads to fighting, blame and criticism. It is also important to look at where you both come from and how your parents resolved or avoided their differences. We often associate talking with negativity if we have witnessed a lot of fighting, silence or tension between our parents. You just want to keep the peace and get on with things. Often, one partner feels that they are not very good 'at that talking thing'. There are many reasons why your partner might avoid communication.

The truth is that you don't have to be a good communicator to communicate. We all communicate all the time, often non-verbally. Your partner may do more and talk less. Doing things for each other is also talking. Look at what is sending you meaningful messages. It is true that you cannot build a relationship on non-verbal communication alone – you will need to have some honest conversations, too, to feel connected.

It sounds like the experience of talking in your relationship has become a negative one. Focus on how you can change this experience together. What do you both need from each other to feel more comfortable during a conversation? If your partner still refuses to communicate in way that you need, you may have to put your foot down and ask for help. If your invitations for communication are denied and they refuse to get help, you need to ask yourself if you can be in a relationship that avoids communication.

Q: *How does one manage control issues in a relationship?*
A: Control is often about anxiety, insecurity and the need for power or calm. Your anxieties and fears will make you try control your environment and the people in it, as you believe that if you can control things, you will have peace of mind. But control has never created calm. The truth is that control creates more anxiety, and the people you control will most likely feel bullied. You can only stop or manage control issues if you name and recognise them as a problem.

Deal with the anxiety that fuels the control. Speaking openly to your controlling partner about the impact of the control on your relationship and sense of self may create some awareness, which could be the first step to recovery. If your attempts to speak about the control are dismissed, it is often impossible to change things. On your own, you could try step out of the control by removing yourself or having firmer boundaries. You need to take a silent or verbal stand against controlling behaviour. This can often lead to conflict, but conflict and resistance are part of the process of change and should be expected. If the control is too damaging and there are no signs of change, it will destroy your relationship.

FINANCES

Q: *How do you manage finances in relationships with single and dual incomes?*
A: Your interactions about finances should always be transparent and honest. Being secretive or closed about your finances creates a break in trust. As you are one team, sharing one life, it is important that you both always stay aware of the money that comes into and goes out of your life. No matter where your income comes from, your

intention is always to stay informed. One healthy way of being on the same financial page is to have regular finance meetings – at least once a month – in which you discuss your income and expenses for the month and all other financial decisions.

If you have a single-income family, you need to come to a shared decision about how money flows between you. It is unhealthy when one partner constantly has to ask for money and the other partner is the decision-maker. It puts you both in uncomfortable and unattractive roles. Your financial decisions are not based on your emotions, but on numbers. Sit together and discuss where you are financially, what is possible, and how you access money together.

In dual-income families, the same processes apply. Make a list of monthly expenses and income, then divide your expenses and decide together who will be responsible for managing which expenses. Divide your expenses proportionally to your incomes – if you earn 20 percent more than your partner, your contribution to expenses may be 20 percent more. This division creates the experience of equality. You need to come to an agreement about what joint and individual expenses are. You need to be open about all investments, trusts, policies and income from other sources.

THE LIFE OF A RELATIONSHIP

Q: *Is honesty about your feelings a good policy in relationships? Do more relationships survive honesty than not? Does honesty ultimately create a feeling of trust? It seems to me that when a partner or family member decides to be honest, no matter how caring or well intentioned they may be, lengthy conflicts and unhappy endings often result.*

A: It is a good policy in any growing relationship to be honest about your thoughts and feelings. As necessary as honesty is, it is not always easy. It may upset your relationship, initially. You need to work through the conflict and discomfort that comes with honesty as you step into a calmer space of truth.

You cannot use honesty as a tool to upset or hurt each other. 'I am just being honest' is not a weapon. The way in which you present your honest feelings and thoughts is very important, and should be your focus. If you speak your mind honestly with kindness and love, and are met with defensiveness and aggression, it could be that your relationship is not a place that welcomes honesty. It could also be the beginning of a much-needed change. The implications of a relationship that does not encourage and embrace honesty are a life of silence and tension, and feeling disconnected from each other as you live your separate lives, feeling lonely in your relationship. If you want to remain connected to each other, you have no choice but to be honest.

Q: *Is it possible to balance your needs and be independent in a romantic relationship?*
A: The happiness of any relationship is about balancing two people's needs. A happy relationship will embrace your individual and relationship needs, and encourage you to pursue what matters to you. A relationship that does not learn how to get comfortable with two people's needs in the same space will take strain and often become unhappy. Balancing your needs involves the needs of three entities: your needs, your partner's needs and your relationship's needs. As your needs are a reflection of who you are and what you would like from a relationship, it is very important not to compromise or let go of what really matters to you. If you do this, you are, in a way, letting go of parts of your identity. It is important to know what you need, and to know what your relationship needs – and to be open about this from the start.

Q: *How do you keep the passion in your relationship, especially after a baby or family trauma?*
A: It is interesting that you put the birth of your baby and a family trauma in the same sentence. The period after having a baby, especially your first one, can have the same effect as a family trauma. It is an enormous change for most, a massive transition that often becomes all-consuming and overwhelming. Many describe it as having a bomb dropped into their lives, and find that their activities and priorities shift and fall off the page of their lives. You no longer have time for your relationship, and time for yourself becomes a distant memory.

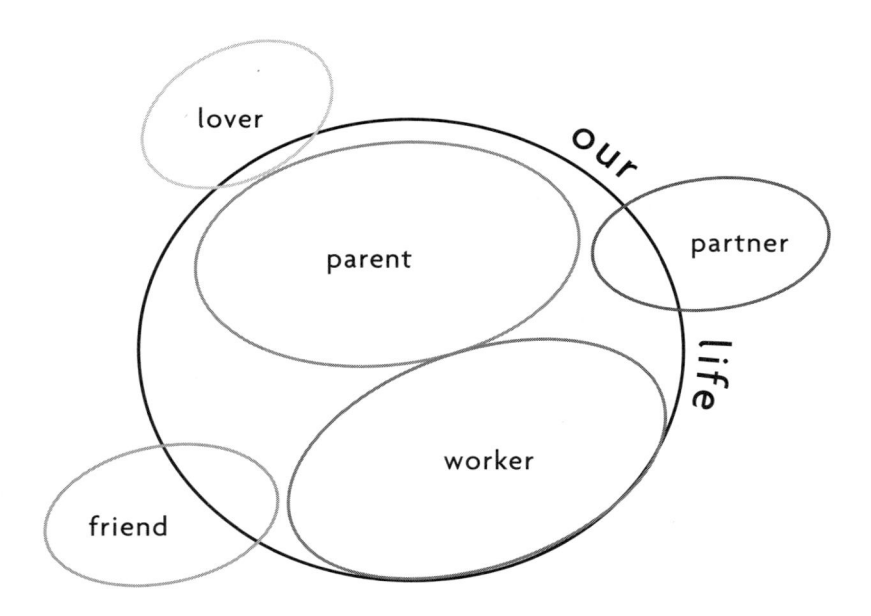

Most couples move between work and their child, for example, and have little or no energy left for the other important parts of their life. During this time, couples feel less happy in their relationship, argue more and have less intimacy and sex. You need to accept this, give yourself permission to go through this transition, and be very kind to and supportive of each other. It is not the time to start fighting, but to team up. If you have not learnt to manage your stress levels and deal with disagreements, it will surface during this stressful time. After a trauma or during any transition, you may also find that what you used to enjoy feels unimportant, as you have changed and grown.

The truth is that nobody will invite you to take back parts of your life, or give you the time and energy you long for. You need, slowly, to take back the experiences of your life that matter to you and plan times of relaxation. When possible, times for your relationship and times with friends or family can be planned in advance and introduced slowly. You need to make space for your relationship and yourself, and book times away to focus on the experiences of your life that matter to you most.

Q: *How do we move from disconnection to connection?*
A: We do it through honesty. Although being honest or truthful is not always easy, we have no choice but to build our relationships on honesty. We can only move to a more connected space if we speak

and live the truth of who and what we are. We connect when we share through talking and doing. The pathways to connection come with honest conversation, with healthy intimacy and sex, and through sharing and enjoying meaningful experiences. When we share honestly, we take the first step in the direction of connection.

Q: *Why the hell are relationships so difficult?*
A: Relationships can be as rewarding as they are difficult, but should never be difficult all the time. If your relationship is difficult most of the time, it needs some work. What most people find difficult is how to disagree respectfully and how to speak to each other when they are upset or triggered. It is also difficult to be in a relationship if you feel exhausted, or consumed by stress. Being in a meaningful, happy relationship requires having energy in you and in your relationship. The more work you put into your relationship and yourself, and the more relationship skills you learn, the better the experience of your relationship will be.

If your relationship is difficult every day or week, it is asking you to give it some serious attention. No relationship should be difficult all the time.

Q: *How do you know whether a partner is, indeed, the one, for the rest of your life?*
A: Knowing whether your partner is right for you requires no analysis or overthinking. If a person is right for you, you will both know and feel it with certainty. It is always a definite, mutual 'yes'. If you ask, 'Is this person the one for me?' or 'Is this person right for me?', the answer is 'no'. If you are doubtful or uncertain, you need to take note. Often, we convince ourselves in our thoughts that the relationship is right. We override the relationship experiences that bother us. We say things like, 'I don't really like this, but he is a good person.' We make excuses, rationalise and colour the relationship with what we want and need, instead of listening to and looking at what we have. When a person asks me, 'Do you think this person is the one for me?', I say, 'The fact that you have asked me is your answer, and it is 'no'. You should not have to ask – you should know in your heart with certainty. A 'maybe' is a 'no'.'

Q: *Why do people experience a seven-year itch?*
A: A rocky section in the road could be the first two years of a new relationship, the year after your wedding, the first year after the birth of your child, and after a traumatic event.

We also go through major personal transitions at the beginning of our twenties, the end of our thirties or the first years of our forties, and when we turn 50 and 60. This timing could be different for everyone but, in the life of a relationship, these transitions generally occur in the first two years, years five to seven, and years 11 to 15. These are periods when we have more questions than answers; this puts your relationship into a period of uncertainty. You should see your doubts, uncertainties and questions as your invitation to reflect on yourself and your relationship, and to do some work.

Q: *When we get married, it often seems like our 'I do's' change to 'you shoulds'. We move from normal human desires to stifling expectations that can take the spark and unconditional love out of our relationship. How do we put our expectations back in the desire box, and keep them there?*
A: After your wedding day you are often filled with new expectations. For many, this is an automatic response, and not always a conscious process. It is also one of the reasons couples find the year after their wedding one of the toughest in their relationship. It is possible that we overlook our differences and human flaws in our focus on the fantasy of that one perfect day – our wedding day. We may make excuses for each other in the pursuit of perfection. Then, soon after your wedding day, your deep-seated and often unspoken expectations of each other, and what it means to be married, come to the surface. These expectations will put a lot of pressure on you and your relationship, especially if you do not talk about them. You now think you should behave in a certain way, so you respond from 'shoulds' and not from your preferences, desires and true identities.

You may think that needing to do some work on your relationship in the first year or two of your marriage is a sign that there is something wrong with your relationship. But it is pretty normal to struggle with this overload of expectations. Looking closely at what, exactly, you expect from each other, and whether you really believe in these expectations, would be a good way to get back into your desire box.

Q: *Through which developmental phases do relationships move once the infatuation has passed?*
A: For the first three to six months of a relationship, you may be in a period of infatuation. As exciting and energising as infatuation can be, it can often also mean a loss of perspective. This means that we see a potential partner through our romantic fantasies, desires and needs, and are blinded by the shine of newness. After about six months we start seeing other parts of each other with which we had not connected before. The first time you have a difference in opinion, disagree, or get angry or upset is often a significant awakening for any relationship. We move beyond the initial attraction and start seeing more of each other's emotional ways.

In my experience, your relationship becomes real as you start seeing more parts of who you are and feeling comfortable enough to show more of these parts. This often happens between six and 12 months, and is the reason some new relationships end at this time. Getting to know someone properly takes nine to 12 months. In the first few years of any relationship, you start practising some of your relationship skills. How to negotiate differences, how to share your minds, how to manage your temper and how to disagree are essential skills for any relationship. (*See the graph in chapter 6 on page 150*).

Q: *What are some of the crisis times couples experience in their relationships?*

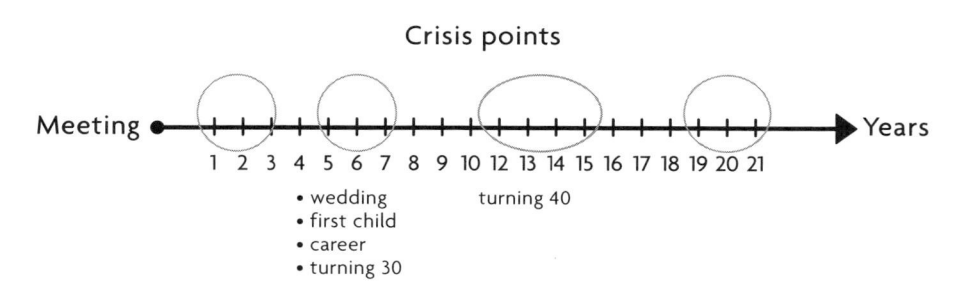

Crisis points

Meeting •——————————————————————▶ Years
1 2 3 4 5 6 7 8 9 10 12 13 14 15 16 17 18 19 20 21
- wedding   turning 40
- first child
- career
- turning 30

A: Most couples I meet find themselves in conflict or crisis in years one to two, five to seven, and 11 to 15. There are many reasons this happens, but often it is about reaching a crisis point at which certain behaviours can no longer be tolerated and need work. A particularly tough time for many couples seems to be years 11 to 15. This is a time (often when you are between 39 and 45) in which you have grown into your own identity, and know what you like and dislike. Your acceptance of what you do not want becomes clear cut. Taking a stand for your identity may become more important than the life of your relationship. This transition in identity may repeat itself in 10-year cycles; couples need to update each other as they change to avoid losing each other on their paths of growth.

Q: *The assumption that always floors me is that each partner should know what the other wants from the relationship. How do you manage this in a relationship?*
A: Sharing your needs regularly is an essential contribution to the future of your relationship. It is at the heart of your relationship's happiness. This healthy habit is your invitation to make changes and to invest in each other and your relationship. It should never be judged or criticised, but always welcomed and embraced, as it gives your relationship a chance to be better. If you keep your needs to yourself, you may be walking around with unmet expectations. Expectations are silent needs. And your silent expectations are hurting you, not your partner's unawareness of what you need.

Q: *Do you believe that people would benefit from courses about relationships before and after commitment? Could they become a norm that may make a useful difference to the future of relationships?*
A: Couples would benefit greatly from learning some relationship skills at the beginning of their relationships. You can learn these skills on your own, often during a crisis or a major disagreement. But some guidance or help during the difficult times could give you some skills that could make a big difference to your relationship experience. Unfortunately, many couples believe that there is something wrong with their relationship if they seek help, or even with themselves.

I often wonder why couples allow so much damage before they make a change. Why wait to make a change when you really need it?

Q: *Are there differences between younger people's relationships and the elderly falling in love? How do relationships change over time and with age?*
A: At different times in your life, your relationship needs to change as you change. In my experience, at a later stage of your life the need for companionship and the simple sharing of experiences becomes more important. In the earlier parts of your life, your focus may be on building a career, sex, building your own family and being social. At a later stage of your life, your understanding of success, love and wealth could shift. You may look back at your life with deeper awareness and insight. There may be differences, but there are also a lot of similarities between the young and old. We all want to feel loved, seen, understood and accepted.

Q: *Why do so many people settle for less?*
A: Our human need to be loved, seen and understood often translates into a desperate need to be in a relationship. The strong belief that you are only complete with a partner at your side makes us accept less than we deserve. We hold on to the relationship despite all the warnings and signs that it is not working. Many believe that relationships will bring them not only love, but happiness. In our desperate pursuit to be happy, we try to fit a round shape into a square hole, even if it is clearly not working. In our desperate need to be loved, we settle, and we wait for that feeling of happiness to arrive.

Q: *Why do we feel the need to work so hard at relationships to make them work? Should we not be happy within ourselves, and let the relationship adapt to that?*
A: Relationships should not always feel hard. They should add enjoyment, pleasure, joy and inspiration to your life. They should give more than they take. But when you put two people's personalities and lives together in an honest way, you need to expect some differences,

difficulties and obstacles. We should adapt to the needs of both partners and of the partnership, and not expect a relationship to adapt to us – entering into and being in a relationship is a huge transition that requires adaptation.

It is unrealistic to feel understood, respected and embraced all the time in any relationship. Even if your relationship is easy, it lives in a context that could have a negative impact on your relationship experience. The contexts in which we 'do' relationships are hard and stressful, so it is impossible to expect a relationship to survive without any work.

If your relationship is hard for a period of time, such as a month or two, it is best to give it some attention. We invest in so many other areas of our lives and expect growth – the same applies to our relationships. We need to invest in our relationships to stay connected, happy and understood. Skills such as learning how to disagree, how to listen to each other with understanding, and how to speak with respect and love are essential relationship skills. The belief that a relationship can survive without these skills is simply not true.

Q: *Is it possible to have one relationship for life? If so, how?*
A: Yes, it is. My parents are proof: they have been together for most of their lives and they are still hugely connected and happy.

Staying connected emotionally, intellectually, intimately and sexually is the secret to success.

Q: *Are relationships built to last forever?*
A: Relationships do not build themselves – people build them. The people involved in a relationship are responsible for its experience and longevity. As with anything else in life, the more you put in, the more you will get out. Relationships have many positive powers, like connection and happiness. Therefore both partners should always make contributions to the relationship's life.

Q: *What is a relationship?*
A: Relationships are places where we feel loved.

LOVE

Q: *Is true love unconditional?*
A: Unconditional love is only present when you both stick to the conditions of your relationship. And, as it is impossible for two people to always know or stick to the agreements of a relationship, love is, unfortunately, conditional for most of us.

Unconditional love seems relevant only in relation to babies and animals. We love them no matter what. But as we grow up, love becomes conditional. Adult love always has, and should have, conditions. You feel less love if you are disrespected or lied to. You feel less love if you are spoken to with gentleness and then shouted at. We love each other in that we try, always, to respect, understand, be kind to and responsible towards each other. The person who is doing damage to a relationship, and who says, 'You need to love me as I am,' needs to grow up. This is not love; it is an excuse to remain a child with no responsibilities, and to get away with damaging behaviour.

Q: *What does it mean to love truly?*
A:
- Love is kind and gentle.
- Love is respectful.
- Love is responsible.
- Love is generous and mutual.
- Love is consistent.
- Love is neither judgmental nor critical.

When you really love someone, you treat and speak to them with respect consistently. You try your best to be kind and gentle in all your interactions with each other. You neither criticise nor judge who the other person really is. Love is honest. When you love each other, you show an interest in and understanding of each other's experiences.

When we feel seen, we feel loved.

Love is not present one day and gone the next. Love tries to be consistent and honest in all interactions. Love gives as generously as it receives.

These are the building blocks and experiences of love.

gratitude

I never really thought I would write a book. My intention was to share the truths about relationships on the Internet with anyone who was interested; therefore, I am very grateful for the opportunity to share my views on paper.

With all my heart, I would like to thank everyone who was part of this book, who taught me about relationships, shared their lessons with me, and wrote this book with me …

To every person who has walked into my life and shared their lives honestly and deeply, I am very grateful for years of learning and inspiration. Nicky Stubbs for introducing the idea of a book; everyone at Media24, who has been amazing; Lindy Samery along with her team of Melanie Kriel (designer), Angela Voges (Editor) and Tiara Walters for a powerful proofread; Anka Joubert for the design input and years of creativity; Gary van Wyk for the photo's and true friendship; All the *Blommetjies* in my life, especially my parents Dirk and Annemarie Blom; Elske Maxwell and Joan du Toit; Lorna Lake, for years of honesty and learning; Prof Solly Leeman for gentle legal guidance; Everard Killian; Stacey Burr for help with the graphics; all my supportive friends; and, above all, my true love, A. Thank you for being patient, supportive, interested and generous. Love you!

S

about the author

Stefan Blom is a clinical psychologist who lives and works in Cape Town, South Africa. He holds a master's degree from Stellenbosch University. He specialises in relationships and works with couples and individuals who are trying to make sense of their relationships.

He has a special interest in the following broad themes: relationship dynamics and patterns, conflict and disagreement, anger management, abuse, trauma, mediation and negotiation, resolution, the processes of connection and disconnection, change, dating, intimacy, affection and sex. Most of his clients are every-day people who feel disconnected and distant from their partners. His work provides practical solutions, direction, relief, movement, greater awareness, understanding and change.

For any questions, please visit his website:
www.thetruthaboutrelationships.com